# WILL THE DUST PRAISE YOU?

To Nancy,
It is so good to
get to know you and
to share all the connections
we have in common,

Mary Sudman Donovan

# WILL THE DUST PRAISE YOU?

## SPIRITUAL RESPONSES TO 9/11

R. William Franklin
and
Mary Sudman Donovan

PHOTOGRAPHS BY SUSAN LERNER

CHURCH

Church Publishing Incorporated  New York

Will the dust praise you?: spiritual responses to 9/11 / [edited by] R. William Franklin and Mary Sudman Donovan.
p. cm.
ISBN: 0-89869-401-9 (pbk.)
1. September 11 Terrorist Attacks, 2001--Personal narratives. 2. Episcopal Church--New York (State)--New York--History--21st century. 3. Church work with disaster victims--New York (State)--New York--History--21st century. I. Franklin, R. W., 1947- Donovan, Mary S.

BX5919.N49 W55 2003
277.47'1083--dc21
                    2003048596


Designed by Linda Brooks
Photogrphs by Susan Lerner © 2003
www.susanlernerphoto.com

Church Publishing Incorporated
445 Fifth Avenue
New York, NY 10016

www.churchpublishing.org

5 4 3 2 1

In loving memory of the dead of September 11, 2001

and

In honor of the living who gave unsparingly of themselves

to those who grieve, are weary, and tremble

Weeping may spend the night, but joy comes in the morning.

—Psalm 30:6, The Book of Common Prayer

# TABLE OF CONTENTS

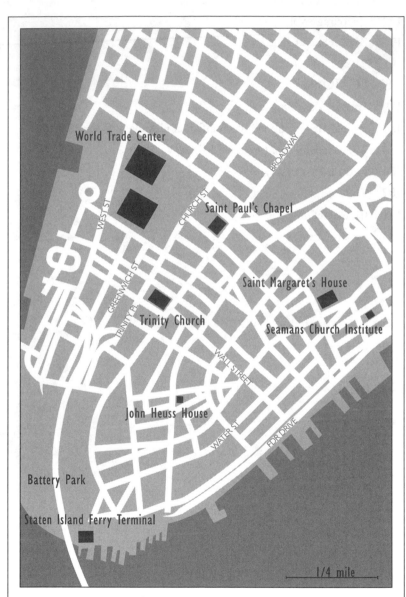

World Trade Center

Saint Paul's Chapel

BROADWAY

WEST ST

CHURCH ST

Saint Margaret's House

GREENWICH ST

TRINITY PL

Trinity Church

Seamans Church Institute

WALL STREET

John Heuss House

WATER ST

FDR DRIVE

Battery Park

Staten Island Ferry Terminal

1/4 mile

LOWER MANHATTAN

# ACKNOWLEDGMENTS

In his preface to this book the Rt. Rev. Mark Sisk, Bishop of the Episcopal Diocese of New York, remarks that this work "*is* collaboration, and it is *about* collaboration." This collaboration has been marked from the outset by generosity. People involved in the response to the destruction of the World Trade Center have assisted us in so many ways—by suggesting other avenues of investigation, by contacting others on our behalf, and by being willing share their own stories and allow us to use their words in this book. We want to express our deepest gratitude to everyone who agreed to be interviewed for this project. We regret that we are able to publish only a portion of their memorable words here. More of their interviews appear in the video documentary, *Revelations from Ground Zero,* produced by Trinity Television Network and on the website, www.spiritualresposeto911.org. The full transcripts of all interviews will be available at The New York Historical Society.

The original idea for a book on the Episcopal Church and 9/11 came from Mark Sisk and his Chief Administrative Officer, Dall Forsythe. They recruited the two of us and have participated at every stage in reviewing the manuscript and contributing to it. Much of chapter two was written and edited by Dr. Forsythe.

This has been a partnership of institutions as well as individuals. The rector of Trinity Church, the Rev. Dr. Daniel P. Matthews was enthusiastic about the idea and brought Trinity Church in as a sponsoring partner, providing support for the book and launching the companion documentary produced by Trinity Television. The Executive Director of Trinity Television is Bert Medley and production of the video has been the chief responsibility of Paul Brubaker, Persheng Vaziri, and Stacey Whorton.

We thank Trinity Television for sharing with us transcripts of interviews taped for the several Trinity documentaries on 9/11 and its aftermath. This book eventually evolved into a multi-media project with a steering committee, on which Bert Medley, the Rev. Stuart Hoke, and Linda Hanick represented the rector of Trinity Church.

Church Publishing joined the project to publish the book and the Church Pension Group agreed to launch a website. Our wise and patient editor has been Joan Castagnone, and she was joined on the steering committee by Frank Tedeschi and Johnny Ross, also representing Church Publishing. The Rev. Dr. Christopher King led us to Psalm 30 and suggested *Will the Dust Praise You?* as the book's title. The Rev. Clayton Crawley of the Church Pension Group has overseen the construction of the website, which will include free downloadable study guides for both book and DVD, a calender of events for the launch of the book and DVD around the church, and links to various sites that contain further information about the church's response to 9/11. In all of this we are grateful for the continuous support of the Church Pension Group and its President, Alan F. Blanchard.

Finally, Professor Kenneth Jackson, President of the New-York Historical Society, brought that society into the project as a repository for our transcripts and primary sources and as a venue for lectures and discussions on *Spiritual Responses to 9/11.*

Neva Rae Fox, Director of Communications for the Episcopal Diocese of New York, has chaired a communications committee made up of the communications officers of the sponsoring institutions: John Allen (Trinity), Marilyn Haskell, Parul Sardana, Paul Morejon (Church Publishing/Church Pension), and Travis Stewart (New-York Historical Society). Lynn Brewster (Trinity) designed the project logo.

We are grateful to G. William Haas and Grace Allen, of the Church Club of New York, for their generous support of introducing the project at General Convention, 2003.

Early involved in this research was the Seamen's Church Institute. Its Executive Directors, the Rev. Peter Larom and the Rev. Jean Smith along with Debra Wagner, Editor of *The Lookout*, have been of great assistance to us as we pieced together the chaotic early days after September 11. The coordinating team at St. Paul's Chapel: the Rev. Lyndon Harris, Courtney Cowart, Katherine Avery, Sister Grace, Diane Reiners, Martin Cowart, Dennis Fisin and Carter Booth shared their insights on the "radical hospitality" that developed there. Bethany Putnam, Executive Director of Labor of Love, helped us understand the principles of relief ministry. The Very Rev. Ward and Jenny Ewing and Mary Morris guided us through the various responses from the General

Theological Seminary. And the Rev. Tom Faulkner, the Red Cross coordinator of chaplains at the Morgue, was generous with advice and information about that particular ministry. We are most grateful to these persons and to so many others who were connected with the many ministries represented here.

We have had the invaluable help, advice, and guidance of the project's administrative assistant, Cynthia Mennell, who has transcribed and conducted interviews, Mary Louise Ball and Andrea Davidson, who have transcribed interviews, and Laura Queen who conducted some interviews for us.

In the end we hope that the spirit of collaboration and good will among all of these institutions and individuals will stand as a lasting tribute to those who perished on September 11, 2001.

R. William Franklin   Mary Sudman Donovan
*The Feast of the Epiphany 2003*

# PREFACE

This book *is* collaboration, and it is *about* collaboration. It is a book that has been composed by a collaboration of authors. But it also tells the story of the collaboration of people and institutions, and seeks to describe God's collaboration with humanity. In that collaboration between people, and between God and humanity, I find the answer to that haunting question, "Where was God on September 11?"

This story is told from the perspective of the Episcopal Church. By the happenstance of history, tradition and circumstance—which some would call Providence—our church was positioned to offer an almost instant on-site response to the terrorist attacks. Moreover, that response was sustained from those first hours through to the day when the Ground Zero rescue and recovery effort was declared complete.

From my perspective as Bishop of the Diocese of New York, the most remarkable thing about the response was how reflexive, how spontaneous, how utterly natural it all seemed. There was need and as a simple matter of course, it seemed, ways were found to meet that need. If ever there was a modern parallel to the loaves and the fishes, this was it.

As I read these stories and I remember back to those events, as I try to see themes and find meaning, I am struck again and again by occasions when strength seems to emerge from weakness. That strength allows quite ordinary people to do extraordinary things. Perhaps I should not be surprised. The Episcopal Church has a long and distinguished history of witness and service to the community, although as a whole we are not a large, wealthy or powerful community. Even the sizable resources of Trinity Church, Wall Street, a major participant in this collaborative work, paled beside the overwhelming need. But those needs were met out of the generosity of countless folks from near and far: boots from North Carolina, pies from upstate New York, money and goods of all sorts delivered via a complex chain of goodwill. Sometimes those gifts were literally passed from hand to hand: from Episcopal Relief and Development, from Seamen's Church Institute, from students at the General Theological Seminary and from parishioners, priests and deacons from parishes all across the diocese and, indeed, all across the church. Just as important were the cards and posters from around the world encouraging rescue and relief workers with words of love and the assurance of prayers, all combining to give the message that those workers were not alone in their difficult, discouraging and dangerous task.

One of the most popular themes in the weeks following 9/11 was the heroism reflected in the countless stories of our New York City police officers, firefighters and construction workers. We had not words enough, so we stretched for new accolades that expanded the vocabulary of heroism. Interestingly the police officers and firefighters themselves often seemed embarrassed by all the attention paid to them. When I gave an award for valor to one firefighter, he remarked to me that actually he had just been doing his job. True, he went toward rather than away from the danger, but that is what he was supposed to do, and what's more, that is what any one of his brothers and sisters in the department did do, or would have done. They were, he believed, simply ordinary men and women who had been prepared and trained to do what they did.

Similarly, the people of faith in our church and other churches who responded with such spontaneous good will and determined dedication also did what they had been prepared to do. I do not mean to suggest that there was any grand bureaucratic plan as to how we might respond to such a crisis. There wasn't. But God does teach and equip people of faith to go where the hurt is greatest and to be there for just as long as necessary, because God must be there and we are God's body on earth.

In his Christmas message for 2002, our Presiding Bishop, the Most Rev. Frank T. Griswold, quoted St. Augustine of Hippo. In the wake of the sacking of Rome by Attila the Hun, Augustine told his North African flock that they were like the bread of the Eucharist:

> You are the body of Christ; that is to say in you and through you the method and work of the incarnation must go forward. You are to be taken; you are to be consecrated, broken and distributed that you may become the means of grace and the vehicles of eternal charity.

Where was God on 9/11 and thereafter? God was on the jets. God was in the smoldering ruin of the Pentagon. God was on that Pennsylvania field. God was in the Twin Towers.

God was with those in and on the pile of rubble at Ground Zero. God was there with the people. God was there through the people. God was there in every act of gentleness and compassion and in every act of selfless courage. There was life, and there was death, in all its utter irreducible ineluctable reality. The message of the Cross of Christ is that both are real and that in both we have a faithful Companion by our side. And that is enough.

Speaking quite personally, I learned from all this that the living goodness of God has been working in us, despite all of our failures and weaknesses, preparing us in ways that we have not imagined for the work that is thrust upon us. Looking back, it is hard for me to imagine how the church might have responded more fully and ably than it did. For months upon months, very ordinary members of our community reached out in compassion to others, spending sleepless nights and endless days sharing in the most commonplace way the abiding love of God for all people. All were served without intrusion by any of the various scars of division that disfigure the face of the human community. All were loved in and through the Love of God. The love that sustained all this work flowed from around the world in a ceaseless stream of prayer, messages of goodwill and material offerings.

I came to see my own personal role as one whose call was to work constantly to strengthen what an earlier Bishop of New York described as "a web of grace." Within our church, that web included: the national church; our diocese; Trinity Wall Street and its chapel, St. Paul's; other Episcopal institutions, including Seamen's Church Institute (SCI) and the General Theological Seminary; and churches, clergy and laypeople within and beyond the Diocese of New York. My role was to help make connections, to provide something of a living link between those many millions of people who cared so deeply and those thousands who were working so selflessly on-site.

That role was prefigured in my experience the morning after the attack. After the planes hit the towers on 9/11, I had gone to several nearby hospitals to await the arrival of the casualties. Ominously none arrived. After a day filled with the sound of sirens, the Upper West Side was eerily calm as we awaited word of other attacks around the nation or possibly even more in New York.

I knew that the area right around the attack site had been declared a "frozen zone." I knew that extraneous visitors, however well-intentioned, would be less than helpful and were, in fact, unwelcome as those at the site struggled to bring a semblance of order to the frantic attempt to find survivors. However, as the night drew on I came to realize that

I had been thinking of this problem as an individual. As a priest, I might not have been needed; as the Bishop of New York, I had real business in Lower Manhattan, where Trinity-St. Paul's and several other important churches and institutions were located. I also realized that unlike so many others, I probably could get to the site because of my office. So I decided to go to Ground Zero. Perhaps I could serve as a "go-between." Certainly I could convey to those working there the love and concern of all the members of our church.

So just after dawn on September 12, Archdeacon Michael Kendall and I drove south. At each of the many police roadblocks we were stopped, our identity and destination checked, and we were allowed through. Eventually the streets were empty and we were advised by the police not to worry about one-way streets but just go directly to Seamen's Church Institute. When we arrived, the Rev. Peter Larom, Executive Director of SCI, met us. We walked with him about five blocks to Trinity Church and then north to St. Paul's, where we discovered that the early reports that St. Paul's had been destroyed were false. We picked our way through the destruction. We talked with firefighters, police officers and emergency medical technicians. We grieved. We prayed. We checked on several other nearby churches to see if they had survived.

We were present; and we began to make connections. And that, it seems to me, is the role of the church: to be in the midst, to be where the hurt and destruction is greatest, because that is where God's presence is most palpable. That, to put it bluntly, is where God needs our hands and hearts to be. We reach out to serve all humanity because that is the very nature of the God we serve. We can dare to embrace this work not because we are wise, nor because we are courageous, but rather because God is with us in life and in death to the end of the ages. That is what I have learned in this work and again in reading these stories.

In the pages that follow, you will discover what others have learned and relearned. I pray that these stories will help us all to serve more faithfully the One who calls us each by name.

Mark S. Sisk
Bishop of New York
*The Feast of the Epiphany 2003*

# FOREWORD

What profit is there in my blood, if I go down to the Pit?
Will the dust praise you or declare your faithfulness?
— Psalm 30, Book of Common Prayer

On 9/11, information was everywhere. Many of those who died in the Twin Towers watched what was happening on their televisions, phoned loved ones and sent out messages on their Blackberries, sharing information almost to the end.

And then there was the powerlessness of words. No words could express the horror of 9/11 and the weeks that followed. No words could soothe the souls of the living. This was said again and again in 2001. No words could express what the city had experienced; no words could convey the collective sorrow. Even when the first anniversary of the terrorist attacks was observed, words failed us. There was, on September 11, 2002 in New York, a citywide moment of silence. There was a recitation of names, and the Gettysburg address and excerpts from the Declaration of Independence. We could not find our own words.

A flood of books on the tragedy has appeared. These books illuminate how our self-absorbed, therapy-minded and information-overloaded society tries to process a national tragedy. And they point up our culture's penchant for merchandising every aspect of our lives, including, and maybe even emphasizing, what we hold sacred. There are picture-book tributes to the World Trade Center, poetry anthologies about New York City, coffee-table books about the American flag and stocking-stuffer books on the inspirational words of former Mayor Rudolf W. Giuliani.

The spiritual significance of 9/11 has not been fully addressed in public discussion. For example, most architects in proposing plans for a rebuilt Ground Zero have been diffident or indifferent to the spiritual dimension of the events of September 2001. In this book, in order to find the words to explore the religious meaning of those days, we have turned to the testimonies of men and women of faith who have agreed to record here their spiritual response to 9/11.

People of faith have always been bound together by the telling of stories. And it must seem odd to those outside the church, synagogue, or mosque, that Christians, Jews, and Muslims, when they come together, should read to one another curious old stories about Moses and Pharaoh, Elijah and Ahab, John the Baptist and the Herods, or the missionary journeys of the Apostle Paul, or the deeds of the Prophet. We believe that the telling of stories has something to reveal about the fulfillment of the divine purpose in the ordinary events of human life, and also in the extraordinarily tragic events of existence. The Bible itself provides evidence that faith is deepened by the retelling of events, because in both testaments the expressions of faith take the form of the recitation of stories of the saving acts of God, and biblical theology is essentially a theology of the recital of events. People of faith have been inspired to understand God's action in the events of their own history and in the crises of their own days, so that they could assert with confidence that the pattern and plan of God's judgment and salvation will continue into the time to come.

The voices recorded in this book tell the story of the terrible days of September 2001. What was suffered in those days will become an important part of the deposit of our faith. But in the long run the suffering will not be as important a part of the story as what men and women chose to do in response.

It is this human response that we believe is the answer to the question put to the future Archbishop of Canterbury, Rowan Williams, in the streets of New York by a young pilot on the day after the Twin Towers fell. The American pilot asked the Welsh Archbishop, "What the hell was God doing when the planes hit the towers?"[1] It is the testimony of the voices recorded in this book that the rule of God, while powerful and revolutionary, is at the same time hidden in and among the needs and sufferings of human beings. God's rule inhabits the dust. There is where God's praise is to be found.

The voices here come together from a wide variety of people and places to point to their belief that the divine presence could even be discerned in the hallowed dust of 9/11. The Rev. Stuart Hoke of Trinity Church, three blocks from where the Twin Towers stood, summarizes all that is to follow in his own testimony.

How could a good, benevolent, omnipotent God, an omniscient God, allow evil to happen in the world? Why didn't God come down and zap things and make them right? Well, I know that my understanding of God is that God was involved in the suffering. God being God is constantly bringing new life out of suffering. My notion of God is that God is vulnerable like I am, so very much involved in my suffering that he shares his suffering with me, which is empowering.

Churches and denominations exist as human communities that search for the transcendent reference point that Hoke describes, the reference point that ultimately gives to lives a special character and defines in a unique manner the quality of human action in response to tragedy. The voices of this book reflect the search for the transcendent as a ground for action in the midst of the tragedy of 9/11.

We began this book as an attempt to document the work of the Episcopal Church in the Diocese of New York as it responded to the massive social upheaval brought on by the destruction of the World Trade Center. We wanted to outline the various ministries that evolved and the ways in which those ministries shifted or changed over time. As we began to interview people involved in this response, we quickly learned that there was no way we could limit our inquiry to "Episcopal" or even to "religious" activities; for the people who carried out the ministries of assistance and relief and comfort came from many faith traditions as well as from those who rejected any type of religious identification. Hence, our ultimate task became focusing on activities begun by Episcopal laity and clergy and noting how those programs were sustained and enriched by the response of a broad cross-section of society.

People responded in various ways. For some, the response was immediate. "I knew that emergency workers would be needed so I went." "We put a table in front of the church and began to offer water to those who were marching uptown." "I ran home, changed into my clerical shirt and collar, and started walking towards the site." Others had a more measured response. " I knew that too many people would simply be in the way those first days. I waited until more definite programs had been established."

Though by far the largest number of people we spoke to came from New York, we also interviewed people from the nearby Episcopal dioceses that were profoundly effected by this tragedy—Connecticut, Long Island, Newark, New Jersey, Pennsylvania—and many people from other parts of the United States who responded in service and love.

With each interview, we learned of other people to whom we should also talk. The excerpts we use here have been edited slightly to prevent duplication and to be more concise, but the words are essentially those of the individuals interviewed.

There are three reasons why the Episcopal Church provided this broad-based response to the destruction of downtown Manhattan. The first reason is geography—Trinity Church was just three blocks from the disaster site and St. Paul's Chapel was literally across the street. Trinity has a particular patrimony: an immense gift of land from the Queen of England in the seventeenth century that enabled it to become one of the wealthiest religious institutions in the world. But it has sought to use its wealth to build up city and nation, and share it in philanthropic and charitable work around the globe. Trinity, a church established by a great gift, has had a long experience of giving to others for the common good, and these old genes sprang to new life after 9/11. "I don't think it was in the stars that Trinity and St. Paul's Chapel should be at the center of recovery after 9/11," said Professor Kenneth Jackson of Columbia University. "But it was. St. Paul's was at the right place. It wasn't an office building. It was a church. It was a place of God doing what a place of God ought to do, which is to respond to human beings in their moment of need."

The second reason for the Episcopal Church's effective response is its diocesan structure, the combination of the parishes and institutions into one religious community presided over by the Bishop of New York. Underneath the high altar of Trinity Church lies the body of John Henry Hobart, the third Bishop of New York, who built up the diocesan structure in the nineteenth century that allowed the Episcopal institutions to respond to the crisis of 2001 as one coordinated family.

The greatness of John Henry Hobart's diocesan plan for the Episcopal Church throughout the state of New York was that he developed both a theological and a practical model of Christianity that could keep in balance, two polarities: the catholic structure and authority of a historic faith and Christian liberty.

The community of faith in which catholicism and liberty were to be brought together in a synthesis was defined by Hobart to be not the parish alone, but the whole Diocese of New York, which in those days included the entire state. Within that diocese, parishes and institutions collectively formed a web of grace, mutually supporting one another in times of turmoil and strain. This web of grace formed by the powerful ecclesiastical structures of the diocese brought bishop, priests, and laity of New York into a common body which could be the basis of common action. The mission of the Episcopal Church was to bring various aspects of Christianity into unity and synthesis and adapt them to a growing city and an expanding nation.

What did the Episcopal Church have to give to New York? It contributed a concept of order that reached beyond parochial boundaries. This network was a source of stability in immediate post-revolutionary America, and it was again a source of joint action in post-September 11, 2001. Hobart believed that this corporate and representative body of parishes, bishop, priests and laity shared in defending and interpreting the true Christian faith and life in a rapidly expanding New York, protecting it from the dangers of religious extremism. Finally, and this was crucial to its role in 2001, the Episcopal Church was seen by Hobart as a community of welcome. In a largely Evangelical America, which prescribed narrow limits on its invitation to fellowship, Hobart opened the doors of the Episcopal Church. He held that Christians should be freed from the demand to subscribe to an elaborate confessional creed; Christians should be freed from the requirement to show evidence of a specific conversion experience; and that Christians should be freed from following one strict code of moral behavior.

No one can discount the relationship of these three freedoms to the rapid growth of the Episcopal Church in terms of both institutions founded and the rapid growth of membership in the first half of the nineteenth century. And no one can discount the direct relationship of this tradition of combining structure, freedom, and welcome to the unique role the Episcopal Diocese of New York was able to play in the crisis of 2001.

Finally, there is a third reason for the story we are about to tell. The Episcopal Church has a history of individuals who responded to challenging times. Individual Episcopal bishops translated Hobart's vision of "a catholic church in love with freedom," of "the church in service to the spirit of the city," into the rapidly changing circumstances as New York faced industrialization, immigration, both Civil and World Wars, crime, addiction, boom and bust. One such bishop was Henry Codman Potter (bishop 1883–1908), whose vision that the Episcopal Church should be the church for all people of the city led to vigorous support for ministries to the sick, the aged and infirm, orphans, and the poor. He created a Diocesan Missionary Society to develop strategies for planting Episcopal churches in growing residential areas, and attempted to bring the church's healing ministry to labor disputes through his active participation in the Church Association for the Advancement of the Interest of Labor.

William Thomas Manning (bishop 1921–1946) served the Diocese of New York during the turbulent period that included the Great Depression and World War II. In the early 1930s, he joined with other ecumenical leaders to protest the growing persecution of the Jews in Germany. He shaped the Cathedral of St. John the Divine, built primarily during his years as bishop, in its mission to be "A House of Prayer for all People." He had a tenement house apartment recreated in the unfinished cathedral's nave so that those who came to worship in the completed chancel were reminded each Sunday of the desperate living conditions of the city's poor.

In the latter half of the twentieth century, Bishop Paul Moore (bishop 1972–1989) vigorously revived the social tradition of the Diocese of New York. He believed that this specific diocesan community which claims Jesus Christ as Sovereign and Lord made clear to all who would listen that the good news of Christ offered enrichment to all humankind. In the midst of one particular crisis caused by ordaining a lesbian candidate to the diaconate, Bishop Moore said, "Biology is not destiny. Through the redemption of Jesus Christ all men and women share in every office of a redeemed humanity. We do not preach a Christ of restriction. The catholic heritage of this diocese—Christ's presence in bread and wine, the human community gathered at the Lord's Table—these things can serve as a spiritual resource to aid in freeing men and women from the stifling bondage to repression and denial and discarded stereotype."

Bishop Moore has seen this heritage of sacraments, justice, and welcome, preserved by his successors, Bishop Richard Grein and Bishop Mark Sisk, flowering in radical ways after 9/11. It was Bishop Grein who placed an emphasis on order, structure, and unity, creating new institutions like Episcopal Charities so that the diocese could respond when the time came. It was Bishop Sisk who received this inheritance and by the quality of his leadership made it live again at the moment of testing. "During a crisis like this," Bishop Moore wrote on January 11, 2002, "the church, clergy and laity, have different vocations at different times. First, the vocation of prayer, trying to sift out our feelings in the presence of God. Then the pastoral vocation—one to one—of comforting the wounded people. We meet the Lord both in prayer and in finding his presence in the suffering of his people. And finally, the prophetic vocations of preaching and action.

These different vocations come and go in a crisis, but each one is necessary."

"But what was absolutely essential," Bishop Moore said, "is that heroic individuals stood up and responded to God's call at Ground Zero. I was inspired by our heroes, all of our people. I was inspired by our church's response to tragedy." It is the record of the choice to act made by individuals of an immense variety in terms of race, gender, sexual orientation, and creed that gives meaning to the title of this book, *Will the Dust Praise You?*

Dust is the most pervasive image of 9/11. Everyone we interviewed about the day talked about the dust—the white pallor everywhere, the sharp, crunchy particles that blinded the eyes and irritated the nose and throat, the depth of the dust around the feet as one fled across the familiar cityscape, the dust clogging the organ pipes in Trinity and St. Paul's.

Dust *was* the meaning of the disaster, for the twin towers, the proud embodiment of all that modern civilization had to offer, were literally turned to dust. The steel and concrete skeleton, the latest in office machinery and computer technology, and the men and women whose work and dreams had made these towers a true center of world trade— all reduced to dust in one long moment. And as the Rev. Dr. Daniel P. Matthews, the rector of Trinity Church, said in his first sermon after the event, "The dust fell all over the world on 9/11. Not one inch of this earth is without dust. Little villages all over the world, people, nations, religious groups of all traditions, all faiths—everybody is covered with the dust of the World Trade Center."[2]

Dust also figures in the title of the Most Rev. Rowan Williams' reflections on 9/11 in his book, *Writing in the Dust.* "All that is written here begins in the dust of the streets that morning."[3] But the title's ultimate reference is to Our Lord writing in the dust. "What on earth is he doing? . . . He hesitates. . . . He allows a moment, a longish moment, in which people are given time to see themselves differently precisely because he refuses to make the sense they want. When he lifts his head, there is both judgment and release."

We close this Foreword with other sermons preached about dust. Augustine of Hippo, a bishop who served in North Africa a millennium and a half ago, turned more than once to the psalm verse of our title as a text for sermons that gave hope to congregations faced with the destruction of the Roman Empire, struck repeatedly by violent invasions of Goths and Visigoths. Where was God, the Christians of North Africa asked their bishop, when the Roman world into which Jesus himself had been born was collapsing around them.[4]

Augustine grasped a handful of dust and lifted it before the eyes of his people. This dust, he said, has been a symbol of death; "dust you are and to dust you shall return" was God's curse to Adam (Gen 3:19). Yet, Augustine proclaimed with mounting emotion, because God has raised Jesus from the dead, the dust of the descendants of Adam will live again. Christ's resurrection brings hope out of the depths of the most radical terror. "Will the dust praise you?" to Augustine meant that faith in the resurrection allows the People of God to take a heroic stand even when all seems lost. Augustine preached that God gives us the choice to look down into the pit of despair or up into the heavens with praise. The pages which follow record the choice that men and women of our time made to praise God with their actions on behalf of those who grieve, are weary, and tremble.

The architect Daniel Libekind's design for the re-built Ground Zero also allows us this choice: to look down into the vast Pit that will be left exposed, the crucible where fires burned for weeks after 9/11, or to look upward to glass towers spiraling 1,776 feet into the heavens. Where we choose to stand at Ground Zero will allow our grieving to be transformed either into idealism or cynicism. Today we stand outside the walls of St. Paul's Chapel to watch this plan take shape; the dust of death transformed by human hands into new life.

---

1. Rowan Williams, *Writing in the Dust: After Spetember 11* (William B. Eerdmans Publishing Co.: Grand Rapids, MI, 2002) 11.

2. Daniel P. Williams, "Dust," *Trinity News* (Fall 2001) 10.

3. Williams, 77-78.

4. Maria Boulding, trans., *The Works of Saint Augustine: A Translation for the Twenty-First Century. Expositions of the Psalms* 1-32 (Hyde Park, N.Y.: New York City Press, 2000) 297-315. In Augustine's numbering of the Psalms, Psalm 30 in the Book of Common Prayer becomes his Psalm 29. SO the exact text reference in the English translation is "Exposition of Psalm 29, Expositions One and Two."

# 1

# THE DAY

*Terror, destruction, chaos, fear, panic, and death—a mosaic of individual memories can help to make vivid the trauma of September 11, 2001.*

*The day started early at the Trinity Church office building, which stands just three blocks south of the World Trade Center site. On the fourth floor, twenty-two spiritual directors from across the United States had assembled to videotape a discussion on "The Shape of the Holy Life" led by the Most Rev. Rowan Williams, Archbishop of Wales. He had arrived early and was gathering his thoughts in the twenty-first floor office of the Rev. Fred Burnham.*

*In the Trinity Grants office on that same floor, the Vestry Grants Committee had assembled at 8:30 A.M. to review a series of applications.*

*The Preschool, on the mezzanine floor of the building next door, had been open since 7:30 A.M. receiving infants and pre-school children dropped off by their parents who worked in nearby office buildings. By the time the first plane hit, about eighty of the one hundred forty children enrolled had already arrived.*

*Just east of the World Trade Center on Broadway at Fulton Street, in St. Paul's Chapel, the eight homeless men who spent each night on beds slightly hidden in the balcony, finished their breakfast, made up their cots and locked and left the building by 8:00 as they did each morning, not to return until evening. Unnoticed in the exodus was the one small window in the stairwell that had been left open to provide fresh air for their night-time slumber.*

# THE WORLD TRADE CENTER

*As the impact of the plane hitting Tower One reverberated through both towers, thousands of individuals working there stopped, assessed their situations and decided what to do. Some started to evacuate immediately, some waited for further instructions from safety officers, some resumed their daily work. Liam Carroll, an executive in the Morgan Stanley office on the seventy-second floor of Tower Two, was typical of many people. He immediately started to evacuate.*

## Liam Carroll—Didn't anyone stop to help you?

I came upon a woman who was by herself and in a desperate state. She was struggling to get down the staircase and she looked like she was about to collapse. I came up behind her and asked her very calmly where everyone went. She moved to the right side of the staircase and clutched one handrail with both hands. "They all ran down the stairs," she said, still focusing on getting down the stairs herself.

"Come on honey, I'll help you get out of here," I said. I put my arm under hers to support her and also to get her to stand upright. I put my hand in hers and grasped it tight and looked her straight in the eyes and told her, "Honey, you and I are getting out of here together! Now let's go. We have a long way to go!"

She was shocked, desperate and confused. I knew from that point on that my job for the day was to get that woman down sixty double flights of stairs and out of the building. I was not going to leave her and I was going to get her to safety come hell or high water. That was my mission.

It was sort of like Job, you know. I'm finally out of the building and I'm safe, but then I have to find an ambulance. When I finally got her in the ambulance and thought, "Now she's safe. She's going to be all right," the building came down. And we had to start running all over again.

But I couldn't just leave her. I told her I would help her. You do what you say you'll do. You do the right thing. I told her that I would help her get out and that we would be okay. So I stayed with her.

*In Tower One, six firefighters from Ladder Company 6 in Chinatown had ascended the stairs and were on the twenty-seventh floor when Tower Two collapsed. Captain Jay Jonas ordered his men to head back down the stairs. They encountered Josephine Harris, an elderly woman who could walk no further, and carried her down to the fourth floor when their building collapsed. The air pocket in the stairwell saved them and they were rescued. They were among only twenty people who came out after the collapse.*

## Jay Jonas—This battalion must leave the building.

Why did I survive when so many fantastic people didn't? I had over a hundred friends that died that day. What does that say about how good they were? Was I a better person than they were? I doubt it. Why was I chosen? I don't know. I don't know if I was chosen. I've had people come up to me and say, "Well, God was with you that day." I can't discount that. But by saying that God was with me, I'm also saying in an unspoken way that God was not with the others. That's a hard one for me to accept. I don't want to go there.

God gave us the courage and strength to stop and intentionally put ourselves into harm's way to rescue Josephine Harris. Our having the strength and courage to do that was also saving ourselves, but we didn't know that at the time.

People should never forget what happened that day. Ordinary people displayed an overabundance of courage and heroism—the firemen and policemen who went running into those buildings. These are guys who are getting a barely middle-class salary and they are charging into those buildings. We knew how serious this was. Before I hit the stairway, I knew we were at war with somebody. I didn't know who. And then when the second plane hit, well, all bets were off. We didn't know if there was going to be a third? A fourth plane? And we hit the stairs anyway. We went to work. And the primary motivator was, there's thousands of people upstairs who need our help now. "Let's go."

*Is my loved one alive? That was the immediate question in the minds of thousands of people who had family or friends working in the twin towers. The Bishop of Newark, the Rt. Rev. John Palmer Croneberger, who lived just across the Hudson in Montclair, New Jersey, shared that experience. His daughter, Rebecca Smith, worked as an attorney for the Port Authority of New York and New Jersey.*

**Jack Croneberger—Where is my daughter?**

Her office was on the sixty-first floor of the north tower. We knew that she was there before 8:30 in the morning and we knew that when the plane hit, it hit the north tower where she was. We were not able to make any contact with her with cell phones or with land phones. For about an hour and a half we didn't know whether or not she was alive. During that time, she was making her way down the stairwell. As she and others were coming down, police and firefighters were going up and it created quite a jam. People were trying to be as sensitive to each other as possible, but it was a frantic time.

When she got down on the ground floor, the other tower went down and she started running for her life thinking that there was no escape. But she did. She headed north and she did survive. Her brother lives on Twenty-first Street and she worked her way up to his apartment and was finally able to call us from there to tell us she was alive. They discovered that there were trains leaving the city so she took the train to Penn Station in Newark. Marilyn and I picked her up and drove her to her home in Princeton. We got to see her reunited with her husband and her one-year-old child. We were obviously weeping with tears of joy and yet also feeling that there were going to be thousands of people who were not going to have that experience.

# TRINITY CHURCH

*David White worked for Trinity Video. He was on his way to the television studio to film the spirituality conference.*

**David White—What was my chief responsibility?**

When the first plane hit, I ran into the television studio, and I grabbed a camera, looked around and thought, "Who should I give this to?" I remember that some people had complained that Evan, on a shoot, had been right in their face. I thought, "I want somebody who's going to put the camera in somebody's face! I want this close up, I want good footage."

I saw Evan and I said, "This is the guy!" So I handed him the camera and said, "this is it, this is your chance." And boom! He left with the camera to go shoot.

My wife had dropped our son, Daniel, off in the preschool, and she was going down the elevator when the first plane hit. I ran into her on the street, and said, "Go back up to the school and stay with Daniel." And then I went back up to the television studio, and I tried to figure out what to do next. I ended up going downstairs, to be with Daniel and Marta, who had been evacuated down into the sub-basement of the building.

We were down there and it felt safe. Then we heard the crump of the first tower's collapse, but we didn't know what it was. I thought it was a plane hitting another building that fell onto ours, or something like that. It felt like we were at death's door. The room began to fill with smoke, and we were instructed to lie down on the floor, and keep as low as possible, and keep baby wipes over our faces and breathe through those. I said, "Get to the wall, get to the corner, that's where the building is stronger." Huddled in that corner with my wife and child, there was a moment where I thought this is the end. This is very likely the end.

Then I was evacuated to Staten Island. And I was wondering about Evan. He went to get close-up shots of this event. I hoped I hadn't sent him to his death. I was genuinely worried about that. Very, very worried.

The next day I was watching television on one of the networks, and I saw this video footage of the second plane hitting ... and then this guy dropping under a truck and then running past the pizza place on Trinity Place. And I saw his shadow in the sunlight, and I thought "That's Evan! I'm sure that's Evan! It's gotta be Evan!" And later that afternoon I found out he was okay, that he was fine, and that it was indeed his footage.

The decision to leave was the toughest decision I made in my life, I think, because there were two polar things pulling me. One was my love for Trinity and my boss, and the other was my family. My family won. But it was ... it was torturous. I lay awake several nights just agonizing over what I should do, but I knew at some point that that's what I had to do. I had to take care of my family.

*Evan Fairbanks was a photographer often hired by Trinity for special productions. He was at the studio that day to work on the spirituality seminar.*

## Evan Fairbanks—To record the day.

I grabbed the camera and went. I knew at that point that I wasn't going to shoot stills. I knew that video is the medium of the moment and could be distributed really fast. So I went with it.

I went out onto the bridge, between the church and the office building. Looking north seeing these streams of people running by and debris falling and people walking back and forth with this really crazed expression—the look that everybody had that day. It was like *Dawn of the Dead*, people walking around in a stupor. Total confusion.

I got down to the corner of Liberty and Church Streets and then a gentleman came around the corner who obviously had seen everything and just kind of started spouting on about what he had seen. He was just in total panic. And then I looked over and saw a guy kind of nonchalantly leaning on the hood of his car listening to a boom box radio, sitting right on the hood of the car. So I initially took a shot of him listening to the radio and then realized what the shot really needed to tell the story was to put the Trade Center, the smoking Trade Center, in the middle of the shot.

As soon as I got my shot set up, I saw a white flash come in from the left side of the frame. I said, "How could they possibly let an airplane into this area? It's got to be controlled airspace. What's going on?" By the time I finished that thought process the plane disappeared into the side of the building, like a knife into cheesecake. And then this huge fireball erupted out of it. It was like I was watching it on TV . . . until I saw that the little pieces of debris were getting bigger and bigger. I realized that I was way too close, that a plane had hit a 110-story building and I was standing essentially across the street. So I took off and dove underneath a car.

That had to be the most significant shot that I could possibly get, the two World Trade Center buildings ablaze. I was lying there for a couple of seconds, shooting straight up and I see that all of this is coming down, straight on top of me. And then people started yelling at me, "You've got to get out of there, things are coming down, come over here." I jumped up and I ran over to a deli where there was an overhang and that's where I didn't realize I was still rolling and the sun was behind me, and as I came running up to this wall, my shadow got cast on the wall.

After a few minutes emergency response teams began arriving and the first people that I saw coming down were a group of firemen. In covering the event, I got shots of some of the firemen just walking by me, going to do their duty, not knowing that all of these firemen that I shot are now gone.

One of the squads was the 288th from Maspeth, Queens. They were one of the first units to respond. So there were eighteen guys from that house who walked right by me and never walked out.

Seeing that I had filmed the second plane, two Port Authority policemen wanted to copy the tape, so we made our way to the police desk in the basement of Building Five. We hung out at the police desk for a while. Nobody was scared. Nobody had any impending sense of doom. We sat there for twenty minutes. Then we headed out of the basement, up through the plaza, across the plaza and across Church Street where I stopped and turned around to take one more shot before we headed down Trinity Place. And Building Two collapsed.

I turned and ran but somehow kept the camera rolling. This inverse mushroom cloud was consuming everything behind me. Coming over the top of Building Five, where I had just been and chasing me down. I looked ahead of me and saw a big fire department rescue truck and dived under that truck. But when Building Two first started coming down I realized my chances were...were zip.

My only impulse was to duck and cover and pull the camera into me and hope that the camera survived. If I wasn't going to survive, I wanted the tape to survive, because I knew I had shot something that was world history.

Everything went pitch black and then it got quiet. Then a couple of seconds later everything was white. Solid white. I got up, almost on my knees and I remember looking down and seeing my right hand on the top of the camera and realizing that this storm had come through and somehow I was still alive and conscious. I was experiencing difficulty breathing because the air was thick with soot and everything else that had been the World Trade Center.

Now I just kind of go on with my daily life. As long as I'm busy, things seem to be okay, but anytime I don't have anything on my schedule and there's a couple of hours where there's nothing to do, I find myself getting kind of down and a little depressed. I wonder why I got to stay here when all those people didn't. I've realized that whatever I'm here on this planet to do and whatever I've been dreaming about doing, it's time to do it, because how many times have we all heard that being in a situation like this, where your life is in danger, changes your perspective on things. People who have near-death experiences say that every day they thank God that they're alive and they try to do things to better themselves and help people. That's kind of the way I feel. Ultimately this event gave me confirmation that what I'm aiming for in life is the right thing. That being good to people, giving rather that receiving, helping doing things that are for the benefit of the world and humanity, versus being selfish and greedy is the way to go.

Maybe, because I've been striving toward that in the last few years, that's why I was given that opportunity to stand on that corner and get that shot and then get out of it. It's really tough to play off having a good feeling about going on with life when you know that there were thousands of people that didn't have that chance. That should motivate us all to do the right thing and take this planet in the direction that it needs to go rather than keeping it where it's been.

*The Rev. Dr. Fred Burnham, Director of Trinity Institute, had gathered the group of spiritual directors who were there to videotape a discussion on "The Shape of a Holy Life" led by Rowan Williams.*

## Fred Burnham— Comrades in the face of death.

We arrived early and I took the archbishop up to the study on the twenty-first floor so that he could have a little peace until he was scheduled to go into make-up. I went into my office and was sitting at my desk when the first plane went in. It sounded so close, like it went right over the top of my head and the impact against the building sounded like a sonic boom. So I sprung up out of my desk and raced across the hall into my study and said to Rowan, "Some cowboy's just gone through the sound barrier."

About that time, we heard Maggy Charles, the grant officer's assistant, screaming because she could see out the windows onto the World Trade Center. We went down there and after a few minutes of watching debris fly by and watching the smoke billow out of the tower, we elected to go down to the studio on the fourth floor where the other people were waiting.

Just as we got there, the second plane went in. We were in the middle of a war zone. As some of the crew began to panic, Bert Medley, the Director of Trinity Television said, "Why don't we ask the archbishop to pray?" Everybody sat down in the chairs that were set up for the filming and Rowan Williams prayed.

And that was the first inkling I got of his profound theological insight into this tragedy. Not only did he pray for all the obvious things, like the loss of life and the suffering and the tragedy, but he also lifted up to God the fears and anxieties and insecurities of people in the room. And that really brought calm back to the room.

We sat then for about twenty minutes, watching the monitor, when the first tower came down. And at that moment, the television blacked out, so we had no way of knowing what was going on except that the building started shaking and then we heard an extraordinary, deep roar. Not knowing that the tower was actually coming down, we thought we were now the target and were being bombed. Everybody hit the floor.

Shortly thereafter, the television came back on and we saw what had happened. By then the room was filling with soot and smoke and we decided to try to leave. The most profound moment of the whole day for me was when five or six of us were gathered on a landing in the stairway where the air had become virtually suffocating. And I began to think to myself, "Well, I don't know how much longer we can tolerate this. Maybe we've got fifteen minutes." At that moment, I realized that I could die…when Elisabeth Koenig, a professor from General Theological Seminary went over to Rowan Williams and in a sense put her hands on him and said, "I can't think of anybody I'd rather die with."

In that moment, we, as a group—five or six of us, bonded in a circle of love that I will never, ever forget. We are bonded for life. We became comrades in the face of death. And there was in the group a total submission and resignation to the prospect of death. No fear. And I discovered for the first time that I'm not afraid of death, and that has totally changed my life. My experience, my every breath, from that moment on has been different from anything prior to that.

Moments later the cops broke in the back door of 68 Trinity Place and screamed up to us, "Evacuate!" I'm sure they knew that the second tower was going to come down. And we went down two flights of stairs and out the door into what was nuclear winter. Everything was covered with three to four inches of soot. The windows were broken out of the cars and it was like the desolate surface of the moon with one exception ... scattered here and there were gloves and shoes and pocketbooks. It was literally a nightmare.

So we banded together to make our way south on Greenwich Street towards the Staten Island Ferry. We were a block and a half away when the second tower came down. And that was probably the third time we thought that we were going to die. I remember turning back to see this huge black cloud tunneling down between the buildings at us. We were engulfed in it. And at that moment one of the women with us froze. Rowan Williams went over to her and put his arms around her and walked her down the street. That was the kind of thing he did over and over again.

And then we got down to the Staten Island Ferry building area, where we sought shelter in a construction trailer. There we met a very evangelical man who decided the thing to do with all of us was to pray. And so he got us all together in this great hug and huddle and he proceeded to pray, not noticing that some of us were wearing clerical collars and not, of course, knowing that he had the future Archbishop of Canterbury in our midst. And he went on and on and on praying but it was a great moment, it really was.

*Nadene Geyer was the Director of Trinity Preschool and as such was directly responsible for the evacuation of the school. Her seventeen-month-old daughter was one of the children in the school.*

## Nadene Geyer—Guard her with your life because she is my life.

When we were in the sub-basement and the decision was made to evacuate, I realized that as the director of the school, I had to be the last one to leave to make certain that all the children were out safe. So I made the decision to give my daughter to one of the teachers, saying, "Guard her with your life because she's my life!" And then everyone evacuated. We came out onto Greenwich Street. It was pitch black outside even though it was the middle of the morning.

As we began to walk, we got about a block and a half away, and the second tower fell. Things started to fall from the sky. There were planes overhead, and I was convinced we were being bombed. And everyone scattered. At that point I lost my daughter and did not know where she was for five hours.

I led about forty children and families and teachers to the ferry terminal and from there we boarded a bus. Since it was going uptown, I asked them to let us off near the Educational Alliance, where I used to work. I knew they would provide safe haven for us. We walked the ten blocks, parents and teachers carrying children, Father Callaway, Mother Silver and I leading the group. We were all covered in white ash. The staff at the Alliance took us in but their phones were not working. I had to go next door to the Jewish Burial Society to use their phones to change the outgoing message on our preschool phone number, telling parents where they could find their children.

I still had no idea where my child was, or six other children and five teachers. About five hours later, they were able to finally get through to us and say, "We are in Bay Ridge, Brooklyn, in a church. We are all safe, we're all fine. We've been treated incredibly well by the pastor of this church." It was the First Evangelical Free Church in Bay Ridge. And then I had to figure out how we were going to get to Bay Ridge. We walked across the Brooklyn Bridge and I called a parent who lived Brooklyn and asked him if we met him at his house, could he drive us into Bay Ridge. He and another parent kindly agreed to do so. I was reunited with my daughter and stayed at the home of one of my staff members.

*The Rev. Gayanne Silver is the Associate for Worship and Education Ministries at Trinity Church. A mother herself, she was immediately concerned for the children at the preschool and knew that much adult help would be needed in the evacuation.*

## Gayanne Silver—Carrying Lily.

I was carrying a small child named Lily. She was about three. Lily was not real pleased about me picking her up. She didn't know me from Adam's housecat, and here I was, carrying her out, trying to get her to keep the paper towel over her mouth. So she was struggling with me. Then we got outside and little Lily looked around at that street, and she put that towel over her whole face, wrapped her arm around my neck, threw her legs around my waist and hung on for dear life.

All of us were totally focused on those children and getting them to a place of safety. Lily's mother was a single mother who worked in the World Trade Center. It was late in the day before we knew that she was okay.

When we went out onto Greenwich Street it was like walking into a video game.

Everything was covered in white and we were all carrying children, trying to get them out as safely and as quickly as we could. We started running down towards the ferry, that's when the second tower went. That's the image that comes to me—carrying that little girl down the street and people yelling, "Go in the middle of the street!" and others saying, "No, hug the buildings!" and not knowing what to do with this precious package that I had. What was gonna be the safest thing? I really thought we were all probably gonna die.

And yet, we were at least together. We were in community. The aloneness I felt later in the day, when I was by myself, pointed out the difference. Even at that point I wasn't scared for my life, but I was alone.

*Catherine McFarland serves on the vestry of Trinity Church and is the Chair of the Grants Committee.*

## Catherine McFarland—Finding a way home.

When the first aircraft hit the south tower of the World Trade Center, I had just begun the meeting. In attendance were Dan Matthews, the rector; Jamie Callaway, Deputy for Grants; and Judith Gillespie, Grants staff member. We were in the library on the twenty-fourth floor. We heard a very peculiar sound; I thought it sounded like dump trucks full of gravel emptying their loads all at once. The rector thought it was a sonic boom. Within seconds, Joe Palombi, Vice President for Real Estate, came into the room and said, "Something is wrong at the World Trade Center." His office, a few steps away, had a full view of the World Trade Center. We looked and could see smoke coming from the top floors of the building. Paper and materials were showering downward and when we looked below, smaller buildings had materials burning on their roofs. I called my husband to say that I was safe. We then heard that a plane had struck the tower. While we continued to watch, the second plane came from the south.

We ran for the door, I fell with others falling on top of me. (I really can now understand how fear creates group panic.) Then we decided to walk down the twenty-four floors rather than take the elevator. Judith Gillespie and I both have bad knees so we were really slow. However, adrenalin set in and we both descended without aid. At one point I asked Dan Matthews how he was. He looked distraught. He said he was think-ing of all the people in the building. Life as we knew it would never be the same. Finally we entered the lobby of the Trinity office tower.

We stood for a few minutes trying to decide the best course of action. People scat-tered at that point. Stuart Hoke said that he was going over to the church and I thought that was the place to be. We entered the church and Stuart vested and began to lead those of us who were in the church in prayer and singing. At one point, someone whispered in his ear. He finished the hymn and told us that he had just gotten word that the Pentagon had been attacked and that there was fire near the White House. I remember saying rather emphatically, "Jesus." Throughout the Psalm readings we could hear rum-blings. Suddenly, the church seemed to shudder and a blackness rose from outside creating total darkness behind the stained glass. It was as though someone was pulling a black shade upward. The roaring sound was ominous. I really didn't think I was going to die, but I realized it was a real possibility.

I thought that we had experienced a bomb attack. I lay down on the floor in the first pew. But, then the rumbling stopped, the lights flickered on and off and there was light inside. Outside was still black. I thought, "My God this is what people all over the world experience every day."

Smoke began to seep into the church. I went into the sacristy. The verger and Father Hoke were there along with a parishioner. We filled a bowl with what water was available in order to soak towels. I found out afterwards that the shock of the collapse cracked the pipes, which resulted in no water in the sacristy. We gave the towels to several mothers with children who were sitting in the pews. At some point we were told that the Twin Towers had both collapsed and we must evacuate the church. Then, some-one from the security staff took us back to the chapel to the right of the altar and down a flight of stairs, which were filling with smoke, and out a door. I had no idea where I was. I could hardly see and could not recognize any landmark. Someone said, "Go left to the Battery." It was impossible to see a foot in front of your face. A yellow/gray ash was in the air—it was surrealistic. Everything—walls, cars, people—were covered with it. The ash was four or five inches deep on the ground. Debris was everywhere.

I began to follow the two women with babies but they quickly disappeared because I couldn't keep up with them. I was alone in a state of disbelief. Out of nowhere a young man named Randy who was a dean at the high school on the other side of the American Stock Exchange took me by the arm and led me to the Battery. All he said was "Follow me." He led me down to the edge of the park at the foot of Greenwich Street. From there, I was able to get on a ferry that took me back to New Jersey.

*The Rev. Stuart Hoke, Executive Assistant to the Rector of Trinity Church was dispatched to the church where people were already gathering.*

## Stuart Hoke—Pray for those who persecute you.

When the rector said to me, "Go into the church and do something," I ran to Trinity Church, and, along with the organist, began doing an impromptu service. Reading prayers, reading Scriptures, singing hymns. At 9:59, when the first tower collapsed, all the lights went off and the place filled with debris. People screamed and they jumped under the pews. And I was just as cool as could be. I was standing up there in front of the congregation doing my thing. I was reading the Beatitudes at the moment, trying to find something in Scripture that people knew, that would connect with them. I had gone through the Beatitudes: "Blessed be the poor in spirit, and blessed be you when men revile and persecute you" and all of that.

As the tower fell, I was reading the second part of the Beatitudes. And that was "Pray for those who persecute you, never exchange evil for evil. When someone strikes you on the cheek, turn to him the other also. If someone wants your shirt, give him your cloak as well. If someone says to you, 'Go a mile with me,' go two miles." And all of a sudden, there was this gasp in the congregation, and a sense of connectedness—not only to each other, but also to God who was saying something to us at that moment that was uncanny. We knew what was going on. We knew that terrorists were bombing us. And here we were saying, "Pray for those who persecute you. Never exchange evil for evil. Turn the other cheek." The very things I don't think I would have ever said, things that go against the American grain in such an incalculable way, especially right now.

We had a young journalist in the congregation at the time and he wrote the next day that was the very first strike against the war on terrorism—a priest reading the Beatitudes in front of the demoralized congregation.

# SEAMEN'S CHURCH INSTITUTE

*The Rev. Peter Larom was the Executive Director of the Seamen's Church Institute (SCI), a voluntary, ecumenical agency affiliated with the Episcopal Church. Founded in 1834, the Institute advocates for the personal, professional and spiritual well-being of merchant mariners around the world. Its headquarters are located in Lower Manhattan, about ten blocks from the World Trade Center site. On the morning of 9/11, Larom was returning from a business trip, coming back to the city from Islip airport on Long Island. Finding the bridges blocked by pedestrians, he left his car in Queens and walked across the Williamsburg Bridge to Lower Manhattan. At a hurriedly called meeting, the SCI staff decided to stay in place and open a relief canteen for rescue workers in the second-floor cafeteria. Flyers describing the building's location were printed and distributed to workers and uniformed officers who were converging on the disaster site. Very soon, exhausted rescue workers appeared, grateful for a place to wash off some of the grime, sit and have something to eat or drink.*

### Peter Larom—What can we do?

I can remember walking over to the site at about two o'clock. Two buildings, 110-stories high—I thought the debris pile would be forty stories high. But it was only two or three stories high, and smoking. I was wondering what became of all the people who were in this building. To walk past Downtown Hospital and see the gurneys there, all empty, all the doctors waiting, and no wounded was devastating because it was clear that there were not going to be people walking out of that pile. So my first emotion was the feeling that many, many more people died than what we might have anticipated. There was also this deadening feeling in your chest of thinking, "What are we facing here? Is there another attack coming?"

Then the adrenaline rush took over. "What can we do? How can we do our small part with the resources that we have, make the maps, get the supplies here?"

I watched one staff member, Anita Mullane, the woman who does our financing, in her dress, with her heels walking through a foot of ash toward the Federal Reserve Bank guards, who were standing there in their flak jackets with sub-machine guns, trying to give them a map, saying, "Here's where you can get some food and some water and go to the bathroom." And her courage was incredible—walking up to them, while their guns are leveled at her, to say, "We have help." That's the kind of bravery our staff showed during those first hours and through that night and into the next morning—just standing up to that and being there.

I can remember feeling proud and thinking, "How do they have this ability? Why don't they want to run home to their parents, their children, or their loved ones, their neighborhoods?" But they didn't. They stayed, saying, "We have to do this, we have to supply this kind of help, because we have the resources."

*Meg Sinclair, who lives near the SCI building, saw people arriving there and offered to help.*

## Meg Sinclair—We just did what we needed to do.

The situation was chaotic. There was an immediacy of need. So those of us in the neighborhood who were here, we responded by cooking and giving of our time to care for those who were working at Ground Zero. At that time, we didn't know if anyone was still alive or not, so there was the immediacy of rescuing life. Amidst all the darkness that was around us, there was an incredible spirit. It was like two ends of a stick. You had the death and desperation on one end of it and incredible love and openness on the other. We just did what we needed to do. That meant we got up in the morning and cooked, it meant that we came over and gave care.

At the beginning some of the rescue workers who came back from Ground Zero would take off their gear and they'd have a plate a food and a drink and we knew they had everything they needed for the moment, but we would still come over and put a hand on a shoulder, and ask, "Is there anything else I can get you?" And their eyes would just light up. There was a communication and an exchange that was absolutely extraordinary. Everyone was coming together. There wasn't any plan, it just happened.

*Peter Ng is the layman in charge of the Church of Our Savior in Chinatown, the nearest church to SCI.*

## Peter Ng—We delivered hot Chinese fried rice.

That afternoon, we received the e-mail from Seamen's Church Institute asking for help. It said they needed food, water, everything. So, me, my wife and my senior warden were the first group to go over. I don't know how we did it. We carried water, we carried soda and things from the church and walked down to SCI. We stayed there for a while but because the first day was all chaos, we helped to pass out notices to the firemen and the emergency workers that the canteen was open for twenty-four hours and it would be a place to rest. Then two days later, we heard they lost the gas and could only serve cold food, so we delivered hot Chinese fried rice. We went to a Chinatown restaurant and said, "This is what they need, can you donate it for the emergency workers?" And they responded.

# JOHN HEUSS HOUSE

*John Heuss House, a day program for homeless people, is located about six blocks from the World Trade Center site. Many of its clients are people who spend much of their lives on the streets of Lower Manhattan. When he heard about the plane hitting the first tower, the Rev. Winfield Peacock, the Director of John Heuss House, was uptown, attending a meeting for homeless service providers at Riverside Church. He immediately made his way back downtown.*

## Win Peacock—A refuge in Lower Manhattan for the homeless.

When I arrived, I found people under a great deal of stress. But I did not witness chaos; I witnessed a community that was beginning to come together to analyze what this meant for John Heuss House and for the homeless in Lower Manhattan. Tragically, a number of staff were in the vicinity of the Trade Center towers when the attack occurred, and saw the planes going into the towers and people jumping from the towers. Not only our staff, but our clients witnessed those horrors as well. Miraculously, none of our clients were lost—during the ensuing days and weeks and months to come, each and every client was accounted for.

We remained open that horrific day. We didn't lose any of our mechanical systems—our electricity or our telephone. Though at first, the air conditioning system was up and running, fortunately, it soon became clogged with the dust and debris from the towers' collapse and shut down. If it hadn't shut down, we would have had to evacuate the site.

At first, people who were evacuating Lower Manhattan came into the facility. We played host to a goodly number of office workers, who just needed a space to catch their breath, make outside telephone calls, get a glass of water, to collect themselves, before proceeding out of Lower Manhattan. But very soon into the day, Lower Manhattan became a frozen zone, where no civilians could either leave or enter.

Gradually, we began to coalesce as a community. Throughout the remainder of that morning the staff began to ascertain how to best to proceed. The paramount importance was the safety and well-being of both staff and clients. Though the air quality was abhorrent, we chose not to evacuate the facility, primarily because we thought we needed to successfully communicate to any of our clients remaining out on the streets. We wanted them to know that if they chose to seek out our services, they would find an open door here at 42 Beaver Street.

We stayed open all night and gradually many of our people found their way here. They slept on chairs, which is normally what they do if they are not sent out to either a church bed or a synagogue bed affiliated with the partnership. Even though we're a drop-in center and don't have any beds on the premises, we do at times allow clients to stay with us overnight. The very best we can do is provide them with chairs.

The staff who were here couldn't leave, again because it was a frozen zone. And so they had to stay with us, too. They made accommodations as best they could as well, either sleeping on the floor on cardboard, or sleeping in chairs. I slept in my office chair—kicked back and gathered another chair for my feet and tried to make myself as comfortable as possible. Obviously it was not a . . . well it was a fretful night!

I worried, first and foremost, about the air quality. We shut our doors though we didn't lock them. So the air quality was relatively reasonable. Lord only knows what the long-term health consequences of breathing that air during those initial days will be. Another concern was what was happening outside. Later that day we did lose our television, but we had radios so we could listen to the news. There were numerous other reports that various other buildings in Lower Manhattan were about to collapse. Would there be a domino effect? How threatened was 42 Beaver Street? That was a grave concern. And then, of course, we worried about the ability of the staff to continue being on duty 24/7 without any relief.

The amazing thing was our clients. They were under considerable stress. There was fear, there was terror, there was uncertainty. They also realized that if we were going to survive during this ordeal that we would have to pull together. And they did. For one reason or another, normally we have acting out, because the population that we deal with are primarily the chronically homeless, mentally ill. Most of our clients have spent an inordinate amount of their adult lives under psychiatric care, in and out of psychiatric hospitals. But that night they realized that they needed to be attentive, and they were fully attentive, not only to their own needs, but to the needs of the community as well. They extended themselves. They were on their best behavior. They wanted to know how they could contribute to the successful ongoing operations at the facility. They came through like troupers, they really did. Because we were in the frozen zone, we couldn't get them to their various sleeping places. So we probably had close to eighty to eighty-five people, including the staff, spending the night.

We have always defined this social service/drop in center as an outreach ministry of the Parish of Trinity Church. The clients are not simply cases to be managed, but they are children of God, they're created in God's image, to be cared for, to be empowered, to be loved and to be nurtured. That original vision supported us through 9/11 and beyond. We were able to reach into the depth of our mission, into the depth of our vision to inform us as to why we chose not to close the doors and evacuate. Because God, through the Parish of Trinity Church, had called us to be a presence in Lower Manhattan for the homeless. As long as there are homeless in Lower Manhattan, we will do our best to stay open and to continue to be a home and a refuge for them.

*One Heuss House client told his story.*

## Kevin—I grabbed the back of a truck, rode it all the way to the Bronx.

I thought I was one tough motherfucker until I saw those towers fall. It was like heavy raindrops. It was raining blood. I grabbed the back of a truck, rode it all the way to the Bronx. I just held on for dear life. The driver finally noticed I was hanging on. He asked me how long. I said, "Man, as soon as you came over the bridge downtown!" I thought we were all going to die.

*David Cardona wrote this reflection for John Heuss House.*

## David Cardona—Lost in the fear.

I thought I was a big man with nerves of steel and a heart of stone. I thought I was a big man that would see past it all. So big and so tall and all around me something much more. A building and a twin fell to the wind, with people wall to wall, a blanket of gray and red, of children crying for mothers who are missing and fathers who will never come home. Mothers crying, babies encased in stone, and all around hands digging for bone, hoping to find a tear or a cheer. People working for all of this year, wanting to find, wishing to hear, a word, a sound, even a scream. Better to have a whim of fear, just another building lost this year. Just some other victims lost in the fear, just some other family needing help this year.

*An anonymous observer jotted down a note.*

## Images of fear.

Abandoned coffee wagon and broken glass. The dust was thick on the bagels. The guy just walked away...you know he was scared.

# ST. LUKE IN THE FIELDS

*St. Luke in the Fields is in Greenwich Village and had a clear view of the Twin Towers down Hudson Street. The Rev. Daniel Ade was the priest-in-charge because the rector was away on his sabbatical leave.*

## Dan Ade—For some reason, I thought about the church bell.

Our buildings and grounds director and I watched the second plane hit. Then we went immediately back to the church, and for some reason, I thought about the church bell. Bells are there to call people to church, and we needed to be in church. So we opened the church and rang the bell for about a half hour. In five minutes the church was full of people. I couldn't stay there because I had to talk to the headmistress of St. Luke's School. We talked about evacuating the children because the school was right next to a PATH station, which we thought might also be bombed, but in the end, decided that the best policy was to keep the children in their classrooms until parents came to pick them up.

I went back, opened the church offices for people coming by who needed to use the phones, and then put on my cassock and went into the church to conduct a prayer service. We did the first part of the Eucharistic liturgy, through the prayer of supplication. Of course, we left the church open after the service and people filed in and out all during the day.

Outside, the streets were filled with people. There are two things that I remember at that point: cars started to drive up Hudson Street—have you ever seen a car drive in a snowstorm and all the snow blows after it? The dust was flying like that, and a lot of smoke. The second thing is: you know, New York is all about your corner deli—and our deli is run by Palestinians. We were standing on the steps of the church and suddenly the police took all of them out of the deli and threw them up against the car and arrested them. These were the people that we get our coffee from every morning, our paper from, we're in there six times a day—all of us—we know all of them by name. Apparently one of them, very stupidly said something like, "Well, I told you it was going to happen." Someone heard that and the police were there in a minute.

# ST. MARGARET'S HOUSE

*Joseph Breed is the Executive Director of St. Margaret's House, a high-rise residence housing about 300 aged and disabled people. Trinity Church built the facility and the sisters of the Society of St. Margaret, an Episcopal religious order, maintain an on-going pastoral ministry there. The House is located on Fulton Street, about six blocks east of the World Trade Center.*

### Joe Breed—We felt we could make it.

We have a fire disaster plan and I unrolled that plan when I saw that fire. I realized that the scope of it was so huge, knowing those buildings so intimately, knowing that we're looking at four acres of fire. There was no way that they could possibly get something like that under control, so I realized that we were looking at thousands of people dying right there and tens of thousands who would be evacuating those buildings. So I called in to the staff and told them to get out our water caskets and start filling them immediately. I sensed that were in for quite a go of it.

When the second tower was struck, I instructed the staff to set up a triage center in our wing. We called New York Downtown Hospital and the police department and explained what we were doing. Then, we assembled all of our medical supplies from our new St. Vincent's Hospital medical practice and prepared to receive the wounded.

Then, with the collapse of Tower Two, it seemed like time was suspended. When that cloud came roiling down on us, I was still in my position outside at the ramp. I called in and instructed the staff to shut down the air system. All of the intake was shut down within seconds. Then somebody said, "Let's shut the windows." The staff ran through the building closing every window. We hunkered down, enveloped in the smoke. It got midnight black. People were running past the building. No one stopped to come in for shelter. They were trying to outrun that cloud before it caught them. I ran inside because it got so thick out there. Then, after the darkness started to lift, the old stragglers who were trying to run through it, were found just holding on to our fence. The wounded and injured started coming out of the smoke and we treated them.

We put signs out front saying "Triage Center," so people would know that we were there, available. I staked the hose out in the front and left the water running, so people could wash themselves down; dust was penetrating everything, so they did that right on the street. The walking wounded were assisted into the building and over to the triage center. By that time an EMS fellow had arrived. He organized the center with the help of two doctors who eventually came from a local hospital, because they weren't getting anybody there.

Four volunteers, young women from NYU, volunteered as transporters. We outfitted them with goggles and masks and they would take the wounded, when they were stabilized enough, in wheelchairs down the streets to the emergency room of New York Downtown Hospital. They transported people back and forth, they made thirty trips, taking each person over, then bringing the wheelchair back to wait for the next person.

We also identified the residents in the house who are the most frail and at risk. We called their families and asked them to consider taking them home and most of them did. I think we had probably eight or ten residents who were taken home—quadriplegics, hemiplegics or paraplegics. The few who stayed, we told them that it might be necessary to take them to the local emergency room, simply because we would not have enough electricity to meet all of their needs. For those with breathing problems, we checked their oxygen and tried to make sure that we had enough oxygen to get through a couple of days, because we knew deliveries would be hard to get in. We don't have any nurses on our staff because we are a residential center, not a nursing home, but since we had just begun this program with St. Vincent's Hospital, we were able to get some nurses to come in to help us evaluate medication and work with the local pharmacy to replenish those medications that were running low. Those nurses were also a great help in stabilizing the residents and giving them confidence that they would be all right.

Very early in the game we took an inventory of the staff and residents to determine who was here and who was not. We fortunately accounted for all of the outside staff by the end of the day and told them to stay home, we'd need them in a day or two, but right now was not a good time to try and get in there.

At 6:00 P.M., we lost our electricity. That kicked on our portable generator, which gives us partial electricity, but it was more than enough to get us through, until I could get a big generator two days later. The residents on oxygen were fine—their oxygen tanks didn't need electricity, but some who needed special breathing equipment were sent to the hospital where they had more juice for that very purpose.

At the same time, we opened our kitchen up and started serving free food and coffee to anybody and everybody who passed by. We encouraged our residents to stay upstairs. Later, we inventoried our food, and broke out our ready-to-eat meals. We also established that we had about four days of food for 400 people on hand, which is what we generally keep. So, we pulled out all of those emergency rations and got them assembled in the wing. Three days later when we had to get groceries, I had to go up on my bicycle on a rainy night and plough through the rain at 2:30 in the morning to get to Twenty-first Street, which was the last checkpoint, to convince the Captain to let these dairy products through, so we would have our milk, juice, eggs, bread and butter. He did and I had to tote them down.

About 10:45 A.M., Father Milton Williams, from Trinity, arrived totally covered in dust. He was terribly shaken, but we had an atrium filled with people and I asked him if he would hold an impromptu service to give everyone the sense that we were going to make it through. He did that and it was very helpful. Everyone was really quiet, some people were crying and most of us sang and joined in the prayer. It was very brief, only about eight minutes long, but it left us with a sense of renewed strength. Much later, the residents in reporting their emotion to the hospital psychiatrist said that though they felt anger, the fact that the staff went through their routine so calmly and so knowledgeably, gave them the feeling that we were not going to have big problems here. I never really thought about evacuating, basically because the population is so old, so frail, we would have jeopardized their lives by doing that. Even though the dust was bad, interior wise, we were clean. We had enough food, we had enough water, we had enough staff, and I felt we could make it.

# THE EPISCOPAL CHURCH CENTER

*Most of the staff was already at work at the Episcopal Church Center uptown at 815 Second Avenue when the news of the attack came. The Most Rev. Frank T. Griswold, Presiding Bishop of the Episcopal Church, decided almost immediately to call the entire staff together and asked them to assemble in the fourth floor lounge at 10:00 A.M. At that early meeting, Griswold spoke of his concern for those who were gathered and announced that he would order lunch to be delivered to the office so people could be together and share their concerns over lunch. Most of the staff called and checked on various family members, then continued with their usual work, stopping now and then to visit one of the community televisions. At the noon Eucharist, Griswold celebrated and preached to a full chapel. "His words were powerful," one participant said. "He recognized the temptation to retaliate and said he hoped we could resist that temptation, that we would realize that as Christians that is what we don't do. He urged calm and a confidence in God's loving concern, but reminded us that God was concerned for all the people touched by this tragedy."*

## Frank Griswold—People of faith are called to be about peace.

Several things became very clear to me. First of all, we experienced a profound vulnerability, and we, in the United States, are not accustomed to that. I immediately sent a letter out to the primates of the Anglican Communion. I got back so much e-mail from bishops in other parts of the world who live with terrorism daily. And what came through again and again was, "We are in solidarity with you…. You have sustained something awful. We know something about it because we live with it all the time." Our vulnerability united us in a very profound way to other parts of the world where suffering and violence are a normal part of life. Suddenly the ever-defended, ever-confident, ever-secure United States was no more secure than they were. Vulnerability was the first thing we experienced. And then something else happened—an overwhelming sense of solidarity. People needed to be with one another. That's why I made it possible for the Church Center staff to lunch together. We needed to be with each other.

*In the message to the Episcopal Church that Griswold sent out on 9/11, he repeated his call to avoid violence.*

Never has it been clearer to me than in this moment that people of faith, by virtue of the Gospel and the mission of the church, are called to be about peace and the transformation of the human heart, beginning with our own. I am not immune to emotions of rage and revenge, but I know that acting on them only perpetuates the very violence I pray will be dissipated and overcome....

Expressions of concern and prayer have poured into my office from many parts of the world, in some instances from people who themselves are deeply wounded by continuing violence and bloodshed. I pray that the events of today will invite us to see ourselves as a great nation not in terms of our power and wealth, but measured by our ability to be in solidarity with others where violence has made its home and become a way of life.

Yes, those responsible must be found and punished for their evil and disregard for human life, but through the heart of this violence we are called to another way. May our response be to engage with all our hearts and minds and strength in God's project of transforming the world into a garden, a place of peace where swords can become plowshares and spears are changed into pruning hooks.

# ST. LUKE'S-ROOSEVELT HOSPITAL

*St. Luke's–Roosevelt Hospital is located on the Upper West Side of Manhattan very near the Cathedral of St. John the Divine. St. Luke's was founded as an Episcopal hospital in the mid-nineteenth century by the Rev. William Augustus Muhlenberg and Sister Anne Ayres of the Sisterhood of the Holy Communion. After merging with Roosevelt Hospital it continues today as one of New York City's major hospitals. The Rev. Francis H. Geer was one of the Episcopal chaplains at St. Luke's. In the hospital emergency plan, his*

*assignment was to procure additional local clergy to assist with pastoral counseling. He*
*arrived to find an emergency response area being established in front of the emergency*
*room, directly across the street from the cathedral.*

## Frank Geer—A fireman's faith was both tested and affirmed.

The city planners had called and told the hospital to expect 10,000 casualties that day. So the first thing I did was to go over to the cathedral. I found Bishop Sisk and a number of the clergy on the cathedral staff watching what was unfolding on the television set in the commons room. I said to all of them, "We really need your help across the street. Obviously this is a disaster and if any of you are able to, I'd love it if you could come across the street and help me in dealing with the expected casualties that are going to come in." Within about twenty minutes that whole group, including Bishop Sisk, were in front of the hospital waiting for the casualties. We all stood around, ready to deal with the people who came. At the same time, students from Columbia University and people from the neighborhood were showing up to donate blood. People from the hospital and the cathedral were working together to set up areas on the cathedral close to serve as blood donation sites.

At the hospital, we gradually realized that we were not going to receive 10,000 casualties. What we did get, because ambulances could come directly up the West Side Highway (which had been closed to other traffic) were the firemen and policemen and EMS workers who were part of the rescue effort. A lot of them had been hurt on the job; some had broken bones or wrenched knees; others had terrible cuts that they received as things fell on them, a lot of them had smoke or dust inhalation problems and severe eye problems because of the fiberglass in the air. Those casualties continued to arrive most of the day at both the St. Luke's site and the Roosevelt site.

As victims came in, we matched them one-on-one with a chaplain or a community clergy person. So a fireman, for example, would be brought in, maybe with a broken leg, and we would send a chaplain in with him as he waited to be treated. Some of the most significant interventions that I had that day were with people like that, just listening to them tell their story. Aside from the injuries they sustained, most of them had seen incredibly horrible things down there. The ones who had been there when the buildings collapsed had seen people jump from the upper stories. That was the story I heard over and over again that day—how terrible it was to look up and see people leaping from the top of the World Trade Center because they knew they were going to die anyway, people holding hands.

The most amazing story for me was from one fireman who'd been part of a team of about five guys who were in the building together helping people escape. He was in the lobby in the World Trade Center, and basically he leaned over and lost his breakfast on the marble floor. As he stood up, the head of his team said, "You head on out, we'll be right out," and sent him ahead because he'd gotten sick. He walked out the door and across the courtyard just as the building came down and he ran for his life. The reason we were treating him was that he had tripped and really screwed up his knee pretty badly. Listening to him and praying with him, I knew he had such mixed feelings. Though he was saying, "My life was saved, I really feel incredibly lucky because I could have been in that building. If I hadn't left one minute before I would have been trapped." So he had this incredible feeling of having been rescued from death, but at the same time he knew that the four fellows that he had worked with all had died. Theologically, his faith in God was both affirmed and being tested at the same time.

*Asha Golliher and her husband, the Rev. Jeff Golliher, who is a canon at the cathedral live on the cathedral grounds.*

## Asha Golliher—The bell gonged. A single gong.

The day of 9/11, the cathedral bell rang the death toll all day long. The bell gonged, a single gong. Very mournful. I think it rang for twenty-four hours. Just one measured gong, over and over.

People gathered at the cathedral—people who lived on the cathedral close, people from the neighborhood. At noon, we had a prayer service. We all stood at the high altar, in the great choir, even up on the steps, not really in formation. Some people were sitting here and there in the nave. The bishop led the prayers. Right away, forgiveness was part of the prayers. The prayers for the victims included the hijackers, which I thought was really beautiful and very bold. There were at least a hundred people there.

Then for the next week, there were nightly vigils, which were beautiful. The clergy read different meditations and Dorothy Papadakos did an organ improvisation. There were great periods of silence and then a priest would stand up and do either a traditional reading or bring in a meditation or something of that nature and then there'd be silence, some music and another reading. They were beautiful. People sat up front, more in community and others would drift in, sit down for a moment, then get up and leave.

*The Venerable Michael S. Kendall, of the Episcopal Diocese of New York, described one incident that happened as he and Mark Sisk were standing at St. Luke's Hospital emergency entrance.*

## Mike Kendall—Turn the other cheek?

Bishop Sisk and I went down to St. Luke's-Roosevelt Hospital. When we got there, all along their emergency entrance, there were ambulances, there were beds, there were those little gurneys, there were doctors with clamps all over their outfits, ready to triage. I think we probably saw two or three people come in with smoke damage, firemen; that was it.

For some time we stood there. The press was there, and suddenly, this young woman from one of the television stations came up to me, and she stuck her mike in my face. She said, "Are you a priest?" and I said, "Yes, I'm a priest. I'm the Archdeacon and this is the New York Bishop." She said, "Well, what does Jesus have to say to us now? Turn the other cheek?" And I looked at her and I said, "Yes." I said, "He said it, he's saying it, and he will continue to say it to us. What's going on down there now is an example of that. We are involved in compassion."

She didn't stay long; she went off to somebody else, but it was interesting. My own feelings at the time were very confused. I am a pacifist. I believe what I said. At the same time, I was obviously feeling angry and hurt at what was happening, but there was no question in my mind that was what I wanted to say.

# ST. BARTHOLOMEW'S CHURCH

*The Rev. William Tully is the rector of St. Bartholomew's Church, located on Park Avenue in mid-town Manhattan, four blocks north of Grand Central Station. Tuesday the staff was just gathering for their weekly 9:00 A.M. meeting when they heard the news. One staff member, the Rev. Mary Haddad, had been recruited for the Trinity Video filming that morning. When she called to say that they had been ordered to evacuate the Trinity building, the church staff mobilized.*

### Bill Tully—Let's get out on the street.

At that moment we realized the world had changed. We turned to each other—there probably were twenty people in the room, and said, "The first thing we've got to do is to get somebody down in the church saying prayers. And maybe somebody can put up a sign on the street saying that we're doing that." And then someone else said, "Well, let's do get out on the street." So literally within minutes somebody went down to the café and got a couple of tables and set them up with lemonade and ice water. And somebody designed a little prayer card. And we were on the sidewalk in front of the church with cards that people could write their prayers on.

In the chaos surrounding the event, there were announcements that Grand Central and some of the Park Avenue corporate towers were threatened. So there were suddenly hundreds and even thousands of people on Park Avenue who had been told to leave their buildings. We felt we could offer something immediately comfortable. The church started to fill up. We moved the noon Eucharist from the chapel to the church, and by the time began the service, there were five hundred people instead of the usual twenty. All of this reaffirmed for us that a particular identity of St. Bartholomew's is to be a cathedral-like open building related to the city, no matter what happens. Every hour thousands of people pass by here without even looking at this church. So we wanted to be out on the street saying, "Here's a little water, here's a little lemonade, here's a prayer card, here are a couple of the clergy you can talk to." And that seemed to connect us with the street.

All the prayer cards that people filled out were taken into the church. We have a prayer team—about twenty-five people who do the laying on of hands and healing prayers on Sundays and maintain intercession lists during the week. So those people came in for about the next week or ten days in shifts. All that week through the following Sunday, somebody was here all the time praying, so that these cards went in the baskets and the baskets came in the church and we prayed them.

# CHRIST AND ST. STEPHEN'S CHURCH

*The Rev. Kathleen L. Liles is the rector of Christ and St. Stephen's Church on the Upper West Side of Manhattan. Just heading towards that church when she heard the news, Liles and her assistant, the Rev. Paul Olsson, decided that they could be of help at the site and headed downtown.*

## Kathleen Liles—Being one with Christians everywhere.

I knew I needed to get there right away and came up to the church and got my assistant. So we jumped on the M5 bus to get downtown. The bus went as far as Thirty-fourth Street when it stopped and the driver told us that we had to get off, so we walked the rest of the way downtown. As we walked from Thirty-fourth Street, we stopped at churches along the way to use their telephones to call back to the church to check on members of the parish. We stopped at Marble Collegiate and we stopped at the Church of the Holy Blood in Chinatown. We got as far as Canal Street, where we were stopped. At that point, I knew I had to go back to see about the parish so I left Paul there and walked back.

The thing that really struck me on that walk was the sense that I had of the wider church, you know the Christian church, because I stopped in where I could find a phone and people welcomed me. To go from Marble Collegiate to the Chinese Roman Catholic Church—it gave me a sense of being one with Christians everywhere. Coming back up, I stopped at St. Luke's Church and used their phone and then at St. Vincent's Hospital to help out there and to talk to the people who were trying to donate blood, and I noted the overwhelming response of people to the clerical collar. They were just so glad that people were clearly involved *as religious people*. I had never before felt that people were so glad to see someone who was identified as a religious person, because usually in New York, they just ignore you. It indicated a real longing for some connection to sacredness in the midst of all that overwhelming horror.

We had opened the church before we left so when I got back there were already people inside. We have morning and evening prayer every day anyway, but we also did a service that night, just a general prayer service. We were very conscious of the fact that we wanted to be a place for people from the neighborhood to come so we did a service that night and then several more throughout the next three or four days. We put a table in the back of the church with prayer cards on it for people who came in on their own when the church was open for private prayer. Sometimes people don't know how to express themselves. We had prayers for the victims, we had prayers for the firefighters, we had prayers for basically every category you can imagine. The church unquestionably became a kind of a center for the neighborhood.

*St. Bartholomew's and Christ and St. Stephen's exemplify the basic reaction of Episcopal churches throughout the city. Many churches had people out on the street giving out water to pedestrians as they fled by. Church doors were open for all to come in, rest and pray. For the first week, most churches scheduled daily services. Clergy stayed nearby for counseling. Telephone trees checked on parishioners, especially those who worked in the World Trade Center vicinity. Peter Ng related one such call.*

## Peter Ng—He was taking a nap.

We had one man we couldn't reach who lived in Battery Park City—he was living alone. We got him the next day. He had gone out to take some photos, then went back to his apartment, and was taking a nap. He was around seventy. I found out that he was the last person in that area. He didn't know what was happening. So he put everything in a suitcase and tried to move out and the police stopped him and asked, "What are you doing? Everyone was supposed to evacuate yesterday."

# GENERAL THEOLOGICAL SEMINARY

*The General Theological Seminary (GTS), founded in 1817 to train priests for the Episcopal Church, is located in the Chelsea area of Manhattan, only about forty-five short blocks north of Ground Zero. The first community Eucharist of the fall term was scheduled for Tuesday evening. The service was held as scheduled, with special prayers of the people written by Adjunct Professor Byron Stuhlman and senior Christopher Hofer. Dean Ward Ewing prayed:*

> God of Peace, God of Mercy; be present to us in the confusion and chaos of this tragic day. Grant wisdom to the President of the United States, courage to all who provide aid; comfort to those who have suffered loss, strength to the injured, peace to those who have died or are dying. Grant that this community may be a source of help and comfort, and that your whole church may witness to the power of your love to overcome death, heal despair, and bring an end to violence. In the name of him who died that we might have life, we pray.

*The Rev. Douglas Brown of the Order of the Holy Cross, an Episcopal monastic community, had been at Trinity Church that morning. He fled with others after the collapse of the towers and had finally made it back to General Seminary where he spent the next few nights. He came to the Eucharist that evening.*

## Douglas Brown—I cried all through it.

To some extent, I was stunned by the immensity of what was lost. Despite the feeling of overwhelming grief and horror, I remember thinking that the one thing I didn't feel was anger. Many of us who lived through it didn't feel that. Anger was such a small thing in comparison to the grief for the thousands of people who had died. I cried all through the service.

# GOING HOME

*Michael Lepore worked in Tower One on the ninety-seventh floor. His partner of eighteen years, David O'Leary, worked in East Rutherford, New Jersey, in an office building from which he could see the New York skyline. During the day, O'Leary's officemates had kept him isolated from the news, not wanting to worry him until he had heard from Michael. It was 3:00 P.M. when he heard the towers had collapsed. A friend from work drove him home, across the Tappan Zee Bridge and into Bronxville.*

## David O'Leary—God cries with us.

All I could see was the smoke over Manhattan. It was horrible. I remember sitting in the car—there was traffic on the bridge—and there was a family in one of those minivans, and they were smiling and laughing. And I thought, "Here is this horrible tragedy and they weren't even looking down to New York. They seem so unaffected by it." And that's how I had always been. These horrible things happen on television and you could turn them off when you want. Not this time. This time I realized it was actually happening to us. It was beyond my comprehension that anything like this could ever hit so close to home.

When I got home, the message machine was full. I went through them all to make sure one wasn't from Michael. I knew that if there had been any way he could have contacted me, he would have. I just pray that it was a quick thing. He was right above the point of impact, so I don't think he even probably knew what was coming.

Mike's family came over. We had all the phones manned. I must have had twenty people in my house that night, with all the cell phones, calling the hospitals, giving descriptions of Michael. It was terrible. It was numbing. It felt like it was happening to someone else.

The first thing I thought of when I woke up the next morning was to call Richard McKeon, priest-in-charge of Zion Episcopal Church. That was the first thing that came to my mind. He came right away when I told him what had happened. As soon as

Richard was at the door, that's really when it hit me—when I saw Richard come in his collar to my front door. I consider Richard one of my dearest friends, but he was there as my priest. I think that's when it really hit. But an immediate sense of calm came over me when Richard came.

We went into the living room and we spoke for a couple of hours. He didn't try to bring my hopes up about anything. He just listened to me. Everyone else was telling me it was going to be okay, that Michael was probably in a hospital. There was a reason why he couldn't get in touch with me. But Richard didn't try to do that. He just listened to me, to my concerns. The thing that worried me the most was that Michael was trapped somewhere.

Of course you're questioning, "How could this have happened to someone like Michael, who was so good in so many ways?" We were at the point in our lives where everything was getting so much easier. We'd just bought our house. We'd just adopted two more dogs. Everything was coming together so wonderfully. It really makes you question, "How could God possibly let this happen to someone as good as Michael?" And Richard had said to me, "At times like this, I think God cries with you." That was such a moving thing he said that I felt more resolved to it in some way.

*The Rev. J. Donald Bane's son, Michael, worked at the World Trade Center and was killed in the collapse of the buildings. For a time Michael's parents and his wife held on to the hope that Michael was not in the building, perhaps had not gotten to work on time. But gradually, the thought of Michael's death became a reality. As an Episcopal priest for forty years, most recently at St. Nicholas Church in New Hamburg, New York, Donald Bane had comforted many parishioners who had lost family members, but losing his own son brought him to the bedrock of his faith.*

## Donald Bane—It's really over. And yet....

One day after I'd been down to Ground Zero, I stopped at the Cloisters on my way home. Two things there really touched me. One was a Pieta from, I think it's tenth- or eleventh-century Germany. And it's very stiff and awkward. The figure of Jesus is almost doll-like, and the mother is a crude figure. Yet there's tremendous grief and also a kind of awkward horror to the whole thing. That really imprinted on me how the participation of God in human life, God meeting us in the horror of life, works for us, and why the gospel is good news. And there's a great sense of deliverance from even the ugliness of that particular Pieta. It's ugly and beautiful at the same time.

The other image was one that I had always looked upon with kind of amusement. It's a figure of Michael, the Archangel, stopping a demon or a figure of Satan. And the ugliness of that, its grotesqueness, had always been cartoon-like; but it testified that there really is evil, not just misunderstood people but a powerful something that is not just sick; it's evil. And the figure of Michael, and the fact my son's named Michael, that's all intertwined with all of this.

I guess that is at least a reminder of the deeper level of what church is, what the gospel is. It's not about being nice; it's about really tough things. And uncompromisingly real bad stuff as well as good stuff. And I can't say that was a new revelation to me; but I've gone deeper into that experience and understood that the only way we can live with it is by God's grace. One of the things that it's underlined for me is about resurrection.

Resurrection is already there. It's happened with Michael, especially when I've been to the Pit when the dust was all around down there. That death is real. That death is final. Except for God's grace. So, the message of resurrection is that it's a radical belief that sits alongside a radical skepticism, perhaps. It sits alongside a willingness to look death right in the face and say, "It's really there. It's really over. And yet . . ." and that "and yet" is where there's real faith. That's when the radical trust comes.

# 2
## THE FIRST WEEK

## OUT OF THE ASHES

*In the first hours after the planes hit the Twin Towers, hospital workers and chaplains hurried to medical facilities throughout the metropolitan area. Unfortunately, few survivors arrived to be treated. By the second day, friends and relatives began to search for their missing loved ones. Chaplain Francis Geer described the scene he encountered at St. Luke's Hospital, just north of the Cathedral of St. John the Divine.*

### Frank Geer—Healing, not evangelizing at St. Luke's Hospital.

Wednesday was the day of the relatives and loved ones, the children and the parents coming to the hospital looking for the people they had lost. They would come with a whole stack of Xeroxed sheets usually with a description and a picture of the person they had lost. They taped them on windows of emergency rooms, saying, "If you see this person, let us know." It was really heartbreaking. The hospital set up an incredible communications headquarters so that anyone calling the hospital or arriving there would be met and dealt with by someone who had pastoral or counseling training.

That second day, I was part of a group of about thirty people—chaplains, social workers, community clergy—responding to the people about missing loved ones. The conversation would always go like this. "My father was working in the Trade Center, and I haven't heard from him since yesterday. Have you got Michael Jones in the hospital?" And I would say to the person, "I'm sorry, we don't."

Then these people would say, "Would mind checking again?" Part of it at that point was sitting and talking to them—joining them in a moment of prayer or going to the chapel, because there was nothing we could do to help them find the person.

The people who came to church right after 9/11 came for healing. They came because they needed a place where they could experience some caring concern and compassion. And the churches gave them that. Up here in Garrison, for the next six months, people said to me, "Thank God you were there on that night, on that weekend. I really was in a place where I needed someone who could hold me and give me a hug. You were there for me."

They weren't people who would continue to come to church. It was funny—they were the unchurched people who were not regular members of the congregation, but for two or three weeks they needed to be held and cherished. They found a place where that would happen. People weren't coming to be evangelized; they were coming to be comforted. By comforting them we did the most powerful and compelling thing we could have done. When people are confused and lost and searching, you have a real evangelical opportunity. But when people are traumatized and hurting, the opportunity is to heal, to care and to love. That's what by-and-large our church and the other churches and synagogues and mosques in the whole metropolitan area did those next two or three weeks. You have to differentiate between an evangelical opportunity and a healing opportunity. When people are looking for healing you heal them, you don't evangelize.

*Just next to the great cathedral, the Rt. Rev. Mark Sisk, Episcopal Bishop of New York, was working from his home, gathering information about the condition of Episcopal churches and facilities in lower Manhattan. Assisting him was the Venerable Michael Kendall, an old friend and the Archdeacon for Mission of the Diocese of New York. Kendall describes their journey Wednesday morning.*

## Mike Kendall—Checking on our churches downtown.

We still didn't know whether St. Paul's or Trinity had made it. St. Paul's looked to me like it might have been gone. As a matter of fact, we heard from Deener Matthews, wife of the rector of Trinity Wall Street, that it was destroyed. Finally, Bishop Sisk said, "Let's go. We're going to go. We have to go."

About 5:30 A.M., I got behind the wheel of the Bishop's SUV. I'd heard that Seamen's Church Institute was open and working, so that's where I headed. There was a roadblock at Thirty-fourth Street manned by a couple of National Guard guys. We pulled up in our clerical collars, and I said, "Bishop of New York." And they said, "Go right through." So we made it through the first one, made it through Twenty-third Street, got to Fourteenth. Security was getting more serious each time.

We got down to Seamen's Church Institute where Peter Larom and Deb Wagner were doing a fabulous job taking care of people. Peter said, "Let's go." So we parked the car at the base of Wall St. and Deb, Peter, Mark and I started walking up Wall Street with Deb taking pictures.

Wall Street was absolutely deserted. The police were on both sides of it, but not on the street. As we started up, it was like the morning after a snowstorm, except we were walking through human remains and ash. We started up this eerie street. George Washington's statue was standing there with a little dust on his shoulder. But he was there. And as we moved forward, we could see the spire of Trinity Church, on the corner of Broadway. And we said to ourselves, at least Trinity is there. Then a policeman came out and gave us facemasks.

When we got up over the hill, I couldn't believe what I saw. I've never seen war. I've seen pictures of it. And no picture can capture what we saw that day. It was this dust that you knew was from brothers and sisters who had died. It was paper. Computer paper. Office memo paper. Everywhere.

We walked down onto Broadway, past Trinity and then headed up to St. Paul's. The only people there were the construction workers. Very quiet. It was eerie. Though there was confusion, they were beginning to try to sort through it. We saw shoes. Deb took a picture of a fire extinguisher from the airplane, sitting right there. We saw St. Paul's Chapel. And we knew that it had made it. I couldn't believe it.

Nobody was there, not that we could see but there was still this horrible smell. Behind us we could see the fire raging. We walked the bounds of the church, and talked to rescue workers, praying with them.

Eventually we went back to our car and drove by St. Margaret's House and our churches—Our Savior and St. Augustine's—to see if they were okay. Then we went back to Seamen's Church. People were being fed there and some people were spending the night, but they were just beginning a lot of their work.

Then we went back up to the cathedral close. That's when we started being in touch with General Seminary and with Seamen's Church, trying to set up some kind of chaplaincy.

*Joseph Breed, the Executive Director of St. Margaret's House, was beginning to search for additional provisions.*

**Joe Breed—Bishop, I'm delighted to welcome you to St. Margaret's House.**

Early the morning of the twelfth, I was at the front desk, planning out schedules and saw these two characters coming up our ramp. One I recognized as Peter Larom, and I had to take a second look at the fellow to his left—it was Bishop Sisk! He asked us if we needed anything, and at that point, I said, "Yes, we need bread immediately." So Peter Larom arranged for us to get around forty loaves of French bread, and we proceeded to make sandwiches for all of the residents and delivered the sandwiches for breakfast. That was beginning of the relationship with Seamen's Church Institute—we were trading on and off. They needed water, so we delivered water to Peter; when we needed food, they delivered. Hand-in-hand we supported one another, both with SCI and then later in setting St. Paul's up. It was really quite a wonderful, very naturally growing effort.

# ESTABLISHING A COMMUNICATIONS NETWORK

*Communication was essential for a coordinated response to the tragedy, particularly because telephone contact with many parts of lower Manhattan was impossible because of the destruction of the Verizon connections housed in the World Trade Center. The miracle was that e-mail often worked even when the telephones did not. Very quickly a communications system emerged: Neva Rae Fox, the diocesan director of communications, distributed information and general bulletins to the diocese; Trinity Church's commu-*

*nications director John Allen was able to post material on the Trinity Church website and communicate by e-mail from his home in New Jersey; Debra Wagner, the SCI Lookout editor reported on developments around Ground Zero; and Mary Morris, executive assistant to the dean and president, became the contact person for volunteers and supplies at General Theological Seminary. All were linked to the New York communicators' network, the press and public relations people from many parishes within the diocese who had already developed an effective working relationship.*

## Neva Rae Fox—What I did was connect.

My phone rang immediately from clergy north of the city asking, "What can we do?" And of course, you're paralyzed. What do you do? You don't know the situation; you don't know what's going on. The news media on which we depended for our news was just as clueless as we were. The phone lines were out. The cell phones that I had been using fifteen minutes earlier to call my friends down there were out. There was no way of communicating, but we knew something was wrong. Very quickly, the calls came out for blood, and I remember that was my first e-mail out to people. At that moment, we didn't know that we were not going to need blood. That was my first e-mail out to the greater diocese, "Give blood."

It didn't take long at all for the realization that there had to be certain points of reference. You know, the General Theological Seminary was a point, Seamen's Church Institute was a point, and Trinity was a point. These were all points where people needed information to get out and in. Working with the people from those points, we made sure that we were connected because there was a lot of false information going around. It just happens. Some very well meaning people will say, "You need to send water at such and such a place." Yeah, well, you know, unless you are authorized, you really shouldn't be doing this. It's all very well meaning, but it can get in the way. Mary Morris and Deb Wagner and I decided who would release what data and when, so that we knew we had accurate information. And that was critical, because that way there was some organization to the response, as opposed to people rushing in and saying, "Okay, I'm here, what can I do?"

The response from the rest of the country, in particular the rest of the Episcopal Church was amazing. I received many calls and many packages from across the country, "Can you please forward these to someone who was affected? Can you please forward these to a Sunday school that might be able to tell us their experiences?" And the response of the Anglican Church was very interesting. If there's a BBC, I heard from it. I heard from BBC Canada, BBC England, BBC Ireland, BBC Jamaica and my favorite, BBC Australia, and of course they wanted to have interviews at all times of the day or night to talk about this. What I did was to connect. For example I connected BBC Jamaica with one of our priests who was born in Jamaica. The same thing with the other countries.

*Mary Morris, executive assistant to the dean of General Theological Seminary, became the center of the storm of activity in the usually serene seminary.*

### Mary Morris—I was so inundated with calls that I couldn't even breathe.

Deb Wagner from the Seamen's Church Institute had taken Dean Ward Ewing to see Ground Zero. She told him about the difficulties with getting things down there and getting volunteers. So Ward offered help, "Let us do it at the seminary. People can call Mary Morris there." I think within ten minutes my name was on the Internet. I was so inundated with calls that I couldn't even breathe. Once Neva Rae Fox got my name and number on the Diocese of New York web page, everyone wanted to find places where they could make offerings of themselves. An incredible number of people called.

# RELIEF EFFORT AT
# SEAMEN'S CHURCH INSTITUTE (SCI)

*The Rev. Peter Larom and some of the staff had spent the night at the SCI headquarters on Water Street, keeping the building open for workers who might need a respite. The previous afternoon, the electricity went out, but fortunately, Stephen Jaskiewicz, who lived nearby, came to be of assistance.*

### Steve Jaskiewicz—Get the generator going.

They had a generator inside that church and Peter Larom said, "Try to get it going." So I got the generator out. Tried to work on it for a half hour in my truck. Couldn't get it going. I said to myself, "I've got to go to Con Ed, down the block." So I bring the generator down there. Five minutes and the guy had the generator going, boom, so I brought the generator back to the church so that way we can plug in our cell phones for power. And we ran some lights, you know, for the church and down the block.

*Early next morning, Deb Wagner and her fifteen-year-old son, Breck, arrived with bags of bagels. She first accompanied Peter Larom, Mark Sisk and Mike Kendall on their tour of lower Manhattan, then Wagner took her photos to the Episcopal Church Center where Jerry Hames, editor of* Episcopal Life, *got the film developed and began to provide pictures to the Anglican community. At the Church Center, Wagner met Ward Ewing from General Seminary and took him back to SCI to see the situation there. After touring the destruction area, Ewing offered the seminary's help in recruiting volunteers and locating supplies. Meanwhile, back at SCI, the Jaskiewiczs cleaned out their refrigerator.*

### Tami Kurtz Jaskiewicz—We had frozen crab legs.

We went over there and started helping. And we took all the food out of our refrigerator. We served the firemen crab legs for their first lunch. They were pretty impressed. And we had champagne. And steaks. We figured we're not going to use it. They need it. So, we emptied out our freezer and refrigerator and took it over there. I started working in the kitchen, and Steve started working on the generators.

### Steve Jaskiewicz—Then the Union Square Café showed up.

Other neighbors were bringing over anything they had. They were like, "I know it's not much, but here's a ham." And, for the first twenty-four hours, we worked off neighborhood food. But on the second day, the Union Square Cafe showed up. A bunch of their waiters and waitresses had cooked all day. And they brought down a vanload of prepared food, hot food. And one of the guys that I assumed was probably the manager of the Union Square Cafe (I later found out he was actually a waiter) got on his cell phone, and spent all afternoon calling friends in the restaurant business, and saying "Hey, this is what we're doing, this is where we need you to bring it." And, within the next six hours, we had regular food rolling in from restaurants. And it all started with the Union Square Cafe. I don't know how they found us, but it was great that they did. It was pretty amazing to see happen.

*The relief effort at Seamen's Church Institute continued to expand. With no electricity, SCI's huge outdoor grills were set up to cook hamburgers and hot dogs for police and national guard units, several of which were headquartered nearby on Water Street. The building remained open with bathroom facilities where workers could wash the ash off their faces and hands. Some people slept in the offices and meeting rooms. Donated equipment—face masks, cough drops, clean socks and gloves—were stacked everywhere, even in the lifeboat that stood at the SCI museum entrance. Mary Morris at General Theological Seminary put out the word that volunteers were needed and volunteers from local parishes began to arrive.*

## Mindy Mount—I came with the sisters from the Community of the Holy Spirit.

On Thursday, September 12, Sisters Catherine Grace, Heléna Marie, Mary Christobel and I went down. We didn't have any trouble getting through the roadblocks. Most of the policemen were Catholic and they ushered us ahead saying, "Yes, Sister." It was amazing. There were already boxes of supplies stacked in the hall as you entered the building and people were coming and going everywhere. Upstairs there was a big room with tables set up, food being served buffet style. All kinds of food that volunteers from the neighborhood had brought in. And outside barbecue grills were set up to cook hamburgers. Everything lit by candlelight—the electricity was not on yet.

Police and national guardsmen were sitting in the dining area. And they kept coming and going all day. I talked to people, especially, who had been down there—to the Pile. Then I talked to a handful of young guys who were anxious to go down—they hadn't gone down yet. Many were shaking their heads saying, "It's worse, it's so much worse than what you see on television."

I stayed all night. The sisters went home, but I stayed through the night. They needed extra people during the night. Lots of people came in but there weren't many volunteers available at night.

*At the canteen, volunteers began to hear stories of workers at Ground Zero who needed food and water but couldn't take time to get to the SCI building. Volunteers began loading supplies—cases of bottled water, ice from the nearby Fulton Fish Market, barbeque sandwiches hot off the grill—into Steve Jaskiewicz's truck, festooned with gold crosses and American flags, and trucking them across to Ground Zero.*

## Steve Jaskiewicz—Coffee or Gatorade or Red Bull?

We started hearing from all the men down at the site that they needed coffee. There were a bunch of caterers that had set up on corners down there. We started picking up their empty coffee urns, these giant urns, and ran them to Chinatown, begging restaurants to make coffee for us. And then we'd drop the full urns off at the site and bring back empty ones, and when we brought back the second round of empty urns, the full ones would be ready for us. We spent all day Thursday doing coffee runs, I think, or Gatorade or Red Bull. Red Bull was the biggest thing down there.

The National Guard, you know, they're not from New York, and they had that down south talk, and they hear me talking ninety miles an hour—I must have been on 20 cups of coffee—and they start backing away from me, they got a little nervous with me, because I said, "Listen, I'm going through. You're not going to stop me. We got to feed the men."

There were groups of soldiers all over the site who weren't getting fed. And, at night, at the Seamen's Church Institute I picked up food and delivered it to them. They were all waiting for us to bring hot food and a lot of other things, like toothbrushes and socks. Nothing was getting distributed properly.

## Peter Larom—We had run out of food.

We were surrounded by volunteers. We had run out of food. We had run out of hot-dogs and hamburger and buns. We knew that the Pathmark had just reopened, about twenty blocks north, and we had trucks. And I said, "But we're going to have to have some money." At that point I was circled by neighbors, many of whom I hadn't really met or known. Everybody reached in their pockets and handed me their debit cards and said, "This is my pin number, just use my card."

That was people taking responsibility, just by handing me debit cards. Leadership was emerging from the ranks. The logistics were easy because everyone was willing to come forward with whatever gifts they had. "God gives us gifts," as it says in Corinthians, "God gives us gifts of many different kinds." One drives a truck, one knows how to get a generator working, one knows how to siphon gasoline out of a car so we can use it for the generator, and one knows how to move through these streets in such a way that we weren't going to get stopped by the National Guard. So those gifts emerged and that led the whole group—neighbors, SCI staff, and then others who were coming from area churches—to have leadership roles in providing help to the thousands of workers who were in the area. Not only firefighters and police, but also Con Ed workers, the Verizon people who were trying to get the phone lines working, thousands of workers in this area in those first couple of weeks.

*The scene at Ground Zero remained chaotic. Many separate fires continued to blaze from beneath the rubble. Smoke blackened the air. Sirens shrieked; men called out orders from various sites within the perimeter of destruction. Uniformed volunteers, singly or in groups, continued to arrive at the site. One such volunteer was Kenneth Leonczyk. On 9/11, he had just returned to his second year at Berkeley Divinity School at Yale University from a summer chaplaincy-training program with the New Orleans Police Department. On hearing the news, he donned his police uniform and drove directly to Manhattan, arriving early that evening. For the next week, he worked in the Pit with the earliest volunteers, doing whatever needed to be done.*

## Ken Leonczyk – Put me on the scene immediately.

There were no positive elements when I first arrived. It was dark. You couldn't see the sky because of the clouds of smoke and such. We were on the piers, which the police had taken over as a staging area. I was wearing my chaplain's uniform so they put me with the police departments. They said there was a choice. I could wait up there with the chaplains or they would put me down on the scene immediately. So I said, "Put me down on the scene immediately."

It was like a movie that you couldn't imagine. There were fires on top of you and all over and this eerie silence and then the hiss of the hose. It was amazing, an emotional roller coaster! While I was there, I felt so useful, more useful than I've ever felt. I was in a bucket brigade. I had a cross on my helmet; they eventually gave me a helmet and someone else put the cross on it. I don't know how or when—the cross was made with duct tape. My spiritual role throughout the whole process was telling people that they were okay and they were allowed to feel what they were feeling—that they were angry and that was okay. I didn't have an answer for why God would allow this. My role was more one of listening, being able to reflect questions about the nature of evil and how this could have happened without giving easy answers.

Earlier, when I had come back to seminary after my summer with the police, I had been worried about the clericalization of the church. I feared that the ministries of social justice and working with the poor were only politics, not real ministry. Watching the response of the churches to 9/11, I realized I was wrong. Many ministers were willing to pull their sleeves up and get into the rubble. And they were feeding these people with such a loving and accepting way. There was no discussion about what political party you were in, no discussion about what liturgy you use; they threw all that away. Their ministry was one of being there for people. And often, especially when the chaplains were handing out the food, it looked like a Eucharist. It was a big line and they were handing out this food and, not wine, but water. You could see in their eyes that they were there handing out the Body of Christ, not just a sandwich. And then the chaplain would get tired of that and just talk to people, and that seemed sacramental. The sacramental aspects of the church were abbreviated; they were different at Ground Zero. Almost everything became sacramental because life became so precious there.

# THE HOBART LECTURE

*While Mark Sisk and Mike Kendall were checking on the churches, The Most Rev. Rowan Williams was on his way to his previously scheduled lecture sponsored by the Episcopal Diocese of New York. Named in memory of John Henry Hobart, the third Bishop of New York, the Hobart Lecture was to be held in St. James' Chapel of the Cathedral of St. John the Divine on September 12 at 11:00 A.M.*

### Fred Burnham—An impromptu Eucharist at the cathedral.

On Wednesday morning, as we were traveling to the Cathedral of St. John the Divine, I got a call from Bishop Sisk's office requesting that Rowan celebrate an impromptu Eucharist at the high altar. He graciously agreed to it. When we got there, the cathedral staff took him off to vest and I joined perhaps two hundred other people in a circle around the high altar of the cathedral. Most of the people were there not for the lecture, but for solace.

The archbishop led the service, but when he got to the rubric of the homily after the gospel, he was totally surprised. He hadn't expected to preach. So he preached completely off the cuff. He went back to an encounter he had with an airline pilot on the streets of New York at seven that morning, when he was walking over to have breakfast with the Presiding Bishop. The pilot said to him, "What the hell was God doing when the planes hit the towers?" And Rowan's answer was, "God wasn't doing anything." Now, that's pretty shocking, but he went on explain that God didn't cause this and God was certainly not going to stop it because God has granted us free will. Therefore God has to suffer the consequences of this, just like we do. It was a short, profound homily.

Just after the homily and the creed came the prayers of the people. Since the Archbishop of Wales was using a liturgical text that he didn't know, he elected to do the prayers of the people extemporaneously. And once again, he showed his theological brilliance. Not only did he speak with a deep resonant sense of authority, but he carefully phrased each intercession and progressively moved through the issues of the tragedy— the suffering and the death and the pain—raising up all of the emotions and anxieties and insecurities of the people there. At the end of each petition, he said, "Lord, in your mercy" and the congregation responded, "Hear our prayer." When he began the prayers, the response on the part of the congregation was perfunctory. But as they began to get into the rhythms of his intercessions and they realized where he was going and how he was touching them, each person began to shout the response. And by the time he finished, the response was like at a football game, it was unbelievable.

I was standing there with tears streaming down my face and I could hear people on all sides of me sniffling. And I could see the Kleenexes being pulled out of pockets and eyes being dabbed. In a magnificent way, he had liturgically connected with the people. It was profound.

We finished the service and adjourned to the chapel for the lecture. After Bishop Sisk introduced him, Rowan handed the bishop the written text for his address and said, "File that, please." Then he proceeded for a solid hour to talk about the meaning of 9/11, just the day before. It was profound. Absolutely profound.

*The Hobart Lecture's primary audience is the clergy of the Diocese of New York, and its general theme is pastoral theology. Rowan Williams spoke movingly about the impact on the personal theology of priests of facing death.*

## Rowan Williams—I want to reflect on death as a teacher of theology.

I want to suggest some ways of reflecting on the experience of the last two days, which might perhaps touch the heart of what we mean by pastoral theology and pastoral reality.

It's a great presumption from someone coming from outside to comment on what's happening here, and my only excuse for that is, I suppose, the experience of being a couple of hundred yards away from events of yesterday morning, and so having quite fresh in my mind, as do others here, the experience of wondering whether we were actually going to die in the next half hour. What I want to try to do today is reflect on theology as a learning about death, and also death as a teacher of theology.

Years ago, a very great friend of mine used to speak about the most important insights in Christian thinking derived from what he called the death cell writers. Dietrich Bonhoeffer and many others wrote in awareness of approaching death. And I suppose, too, that I have learned something of this by reading, for example, many of the novels of

Iris Murdoch, God rest her, who was much preoccupied with what it is like to die.

It seems to me that when we are faced with a real, concrete possibility that death is going to happen to us, we immediately have one of the deepest possible challenges posed to the way in which we think about ourselves. We're brought up against a situation in which we have no ability at all to change the future. If the powerlessness is real, and if you're prepared to look it in the face, what happens?

Our Buddhist friends tell us that when we've learned to let go of the craving to leave our thumbprint on the wall, what is left is compassion. Because when we are released from the urge to leave that thumbprint, to scribble that signature on the wall, the urge to act so as to seem to be making a difference, a space is created. A space that is otherwise occupied by anxiety becomes vacant space into which someone else's reality may come.

I want to suggest that ultimately all authentic pastoral activity has to be activity in the face of death. All authentic pastoralness is activity in which, with God's grace, somehow or other a space is made, a breach in the wall of our anxiety and our urgent longing to get on top of things. When that breach is made, and there is room, death teaches us. If we can't control the future, we can't impose the pattern that we like upon it, what is there to do? We can rage or we can laugh, since that is the choice that death puts before us.

## Fred Burnham—That was precisely what had happened to me.

What the archbishop said fit with my transformative experience the day before, telling us that the apprehension of death and the experience of radical vulnerability are the two foundations of any authentic pastoral ministry. Meaning, as he explained it, it is only when you have faced your own death, experienced your own mortality, been through that kind of suffering experience, that terrible, frightful experience, that you are capable of understanding the pain and suffering of others. That, he was telling us, is the key sort of transformative moment in a person's pastoral life.

Now that was precisely what had happened to me the day before on that landing when I faced my death and discovered I was not afraid of it. That experience had broken open my heart and my compassion. And that experience led me to volunteer at the very first opportunity at St. Paul's, provoking me to give my time and my love and my compassion to this extraordinary event that was going on there.

The work at St. Paul's was a totally transformative experience, not just for me, but for countless volunteers who came there, for countless firemen and policemen. It was one of those moments in our history where the Episcopal Church acquitted itself extraordinarily well, and provided a model of what the church could and should be. I am committed now to trying to figure out how you can take that crisis experience and normalize it in the everyday life of a parish.

## Rowan Williams—How do we talk, how do we make sense?

I live in a bilingual culture and one of the difficulties that I sometimes face is what language to process something in. On the telephone this morning, one of the journalists from the UK contacted me and said "hello" with an intonation that told me immediately he was going to speak Welsh to me, and so I replied in Welsh. By doing so, I was saying, "This is the language, agreeing that it's all right to speak Welsh." And if I answer in my most flawless Oxford English, "Good morning," I say, "We don't speak Welsh, this is not how we go on."

Now when indiscriminate violence is met with indiscriminate violence, it's a transaction in language. I'm saying, "This is how we go on. This is how we make sense. These are the terms on which we are agreeing to be together. I understand this language and I'm fairly comfortable with it." So if the first word spoken is an indiscriminate slaughter, if the first word spoken is the sad but inevitable cost to the innocent and I reply in that language, I'm saying "This is how we go on. This is our currency." Again and again in human transactions at every level, personal, communal, interracial, intergender, international, the question of what language we are going to speak together is one of the most important moral issues that we have. Do we want the conversation to continue and in what terms? And when there is pressure for the release of tension for retaliation, that is perhaps one of the moral questions a Christian might want to address. How do we talk, how do we make sense?

*On the second day, other priests began counseling grieving relatives of the missing. The Rev. Lloyd Prator, rector of St. John's in the Village, had spent the first day at St. Vincent's Hospital. On the second day, the relatives began to search for their loved ones.*

## Lloyd Prator—Grief counseling at St. Vincent's Hospital.

I talked to a young woman who was in her very early thirties. She had been married about a year and a half to a man who worked at Cantor Fitzgerald. Of course, you know all those people died instantly. They were planning on starting a family. She was a beautiful young woman. She sent her friend over to me and her friend said, "Are you an honest-to-gosh priest?" I said I was, and asked what I could do, and she said, "My friend wants to talk to you." She took me over there and as I sat down next to her, she said very first thing, "I don't want you to tell me that everything is going to be all right." I said, "Well, you know I'm not, because I don't think it is." I spent about an hour with her. She told me that when she had gotten home the night before, the day of the terrorist attacks, there was a voicemail from her husband which went something like this: "Honey, I just got to work and something really terrible has happened and there is a lot of smoke, but I . . ." Can you imagine? It was heartbreaking. And the saddest thing was that this was a story that was duplicated many times over.

Later I sat next to a couple whose son had worked in one of the restaurants, and they were clutching a little Polaroid picture of him, taken at a family gathering. They were holding onto it for dear life, as if that was all they had left. Of course the truth of the matter is, that was right—that was all that they had left. It was horribly, horribly sad.

*Since the police blockade in Lower Manhattan extended around Trinity Church, the building could not be opened. As the week wore on, Trinity's officers began to worry about where the congregation would worship on Sunday. The Rev. Samuel Johnson Howard, Vicar of Trinity, recalled those discussions, which resulted in an ecumenical breakthrough.*

## John Howard—Where will Trinity Parish worship?

For the first ten days after 9/11, my wife, Marie, and I stayed in a friend's apartment. Marie had her cell phone and I pretty much stayed on it for the next three days, talking to members of the staff, members of the congregation. The first big job was to let everybody know that everybody else was okay, as far as the congregation and staff went. Number two was touching base with other members of the staff and vestry members, talking to them about what was going on down here, and what we were trying to do to make arrangements.

We were also organizing the first worship service since the attacks. Trinity was still sealed off by the police. At 9 o'clock on that first Saturday evening, I had a conference call staff meeting. Up to that time, we had planned to worship at St. Augustine's, an Episcopal church on the Lower East Side. It's a former Trinity chapel and they're part of our clericus family here. Errol Harvey, the rector at St. Augustine's, had very generously invited us. But our staff became concerned about whether people would be able to find it.

David Jette, our verger, reminded me that months before, Trinity had joined in the celebration of the twenty-fifth anniversary of the consecration of Mother Seton as a Roman Catholic saint. And there was a lot of talk around that time about a connection between Roman Catholics and Episcopalians in Lower Manhattan. Elizabeth Seton grew up as an Episcopalian in Trinity Church before she became a Roman Catholic, so she is in some way a bridge between the two churches. When David said on the phone, "I wonder if the Seton Shrine would be available?" I put the conference call on hold, got to another phone, and called Father Peter Meehan. It was 9:30 Saturday night, and we asked him if we could worship there on Sunday. He was very hospitable, very amenable to it. We set 2:00 P.M. on Sunday as the time, and I got back on the conference call. We put together a telephone tree and called everybody in the congregation that we could reach.

It worked. We had a full church, choir and everything, and worshiped there for more than two months.

# THE GENERAL THEOLOGICAL SEMINARY (GTS) ORGANIZES VOLUNTEERS

*General Theological Seminary's fall term began September 10, 2001. Since the GTS campus at Ninth Avenue and Twentieth Street was out of the so-called "frozen zone," that stretched from Canal Street south to the Battery, but close enough to be an important staging area, seminarians and staff quickly began to coordinate deliveries of supplies and volunteers. Ward Ewing, dean and president of the Seminary, describes the evolution of that ministry.*

## Ward Ewing—GTS stands ready to help.

We started picking up food and bringing it down to Seamen's Church Institute. The folks there were doing what they could. They had one generator and a lot of candles and food in the cooler. They needed food and they needed cell phone chargers. A group of four or five of us picked up some of both, and walked down from Fourteenth Street.

I asked Peter Larom what he needed. He told me that they needed some volunteers and that they should bring food. So from Wednesday night at least through Sunday, we were bringing volunteers from the seminary to take shifts at Seamen's Church.

Union Square Cafe had been getting food down to SCI, but they were out of food. Deb Wagner called and said they had arranged to pick up some food at some restaurants in midtown and asked if we could get our van there. We had a red van—a '92 model with 120,000 miles on it—that looked official and it did help us get through some of the checkpoints. By Wednesday night, the communications department at General Seminary had also written up and laminated individual passes that said "Official Volunteer, General Seminary, Seamen's Church Institute" which we provided for all the volunteers.

As Dean, I had to give some clear direction to the students. Such direction was called for when new students, who had attended exactly two classes at seminary, decided that there was a need for chaplains at St. Vincent's Hospital. They were ready to stick collars on and go down to be chaplains. I literally had to stand at the front door and say, "No, you can't do that." That would have been too rough on them, and it would have been inappropriate for whoever they were talking to. Some of those students were among the first volunteers who came downtown to hand out water. If you can't be a chaplain, you can hand out water.

*One of the earliest volunteers at General Seminary was Mary O'Shaughnessy, a parishioner at St. Luke in the Fields, who arrived there the day after the attack to see how she could be of help.*

## Mary O'Shaughnessy—The search for resources.

We needed to get pots downtown, and you couldn't drive there, but they needed big pots to boil water for the steam table. I thought, "Now where am I going to get somebody who would carry a big pot?" So I called the New York Sports Club on Seventh Avenue and I said, "Can I talk to the personal trainers?" I got this guy named Joe, who said, "Sure, I'll carry a pot," and he went over to pick them up. He called me back and said, "Thank you so much for calling us, please, please call us back. We want to do more." So, it was a matter of picking up the phone and saying, "Hi you don't know me, I need help," and people responded.

The seminary students were constantly going back and forth to Ground Zero. One of the seminarians was a young man name Brad Dyche. He was in Oklahoma City as a lay chaplain during the Oklahoma City bombing. He was telling the other seminarians, "Look, you do not have the capability, on one unit of Clinical Pastoral Education, to go down there and try to minister." He said, "I've been through this. I wasn't ready, and I'm still not ready." So he really had the moral authority and the sense to say, "Don't go there and try to play chaplain."

*Along with Mary O'Shaughnessy, two other volunteers also arrived at General Seminary and became the scheduling team. Mary Louise Ball was a member of Grace Church, eager to help the recovery effort but reluctant to be at Ground Zero because she was pregnant and feared the air quality might harm her baby. JoAnne Ciacciarelli was a portfolio manager who had recently lost her job in a corporate downsizing. Though she was a Roman Catholic, someone had told her that volunteers were needed at the Episcopal seminary so she walked through the door and said, "Can I help?" Together, these women began to set up an organized scheduling system.*

## Mary Louise Ball—Setting up a scheduling system.

What was so beautiful about the effort was that the three of us said, "Okay, we need to get this place organized." There was no competition, there was no hierarchy, and there was no territoriality about the way we worked. We were absolute equals. The three of us had the best time working together. We said, "Okay, this blackboard needs to be better organized. It's completely jumbled. When someone calls up on the phone and wants to know what shifts are available, it's hard for us to see." Then one of us said, "I'll do that." So we took sheets of paper and started writing down things like, "September 18—the morning shift is taken, evening's free." And we methodically re-organized all the available time slots. We typed a standard shift sheet and made copies. We got a logbook, and eventually erased the blackboard and got it all on paper. Then we got computerized.

We made a standard fact sheet, so when people called in, we'd get certain information from them, such as: what parish are you from, how many people want to volunteer, who's the contact person, what's their phone number, where can you be picked up, and so on. Then we read them instructions from our fact sheet, so they were prepared when they showed up on site: no children under eighteen, no one with asthma, don't wear contact lenses, and so on. It really felt like a war room—it was very intense.

We realized almost immediately that we could not deal with individual people, there were too many. We needed to deal with groups. Volunteers called us from New York, New Jersey, and Connecticut. Though most came from Episcopal churches, others came from other denominations, or temples and synagogues; still others formed their own independent groups. They didn't have to be Christian, didn't have to be from a church at all. We tried to make that clear. We didn't give priority to any group—"If you call us up, if you can get twelve people together, if you can be here at a certain time, if you don't mind the twelve-hour shift, and you can take one of the spots that are available, you're in."

At one point early on, we called Episcopal schools, getting them send artwork from children. Eventually things were coming from all over the world, St. Paul's was totally filled. We asked people who called in to do things—we got thousands of little kits that contained razors and deodorant, moisturizer, Chap Stick, Band-Aids, things like that and a note from a child was tucked in each one of them. We had Hershey Bars, any kind of chocolate bar, because the workers wanted chocolate, and we had children wrap the bars in notes they'd written. Those were ones that were gone first because workers wanted the notes from the children.

*In spite of the stress and workload, Mary Morris and her colleagues found great satisfaction in coordinating volunteers.*

## Mary Morris—We never knew what to expect.

One day Hannah Griswold, daughter of the Presiding Bishop, got the call about needing boots because the rescue workers' boots were melting from the fires at Ground Zero. She started calling places and about three days later a truck arrived from North Carolina with two young guys driving it. They arrived on Saturday at about midnight and the only phone number they had was Mary O'Shaughnessy's cell phone. They woke her up, and she told them how to get down to Ground Zero, what to say to get through the roadblocks. They arrived at St. Paul's at about 1:00 A.M. and immediately they were greeted by a standing ovation from all the workers at Ground Zero. They were amazingly grateful. And then a body was found—I believe a firefighter or a police officer—and the drivers were asked if they wanted to watch the recovery. I think that was the first time one of our lay volunteers was really exposed to the entire nature of the ritual, wrapping the body in the flag. Just to be in the midst of it was very life-giving.

We were involved in scheduling volunteers at St. Paul's until October 5, and then Trinity came one day and took over.

*Dominick Ferraro, who works for Seamen's Church Institute is a New Yorker—born and brought up in the neighborhood of the Fulton Fish Market. Day and night during the first two weeks, with an American flag tied around his head, he was a part of the SCI effort, transporting supplies and equipment back and forth between SCI and St. Paul's. He also recalls the delivery of the boots.*

## Dominick Ferraro—The boots arrived at St. Paul's

I remember going down to the pile one morning and I asked the guys what they needed. They told me they needed construction boots. So when I got back to SCI, everybody had cell phones and they used to ask me what was needed down there. I told them, "They need boots." It was eight o'clock in the morning. Somebody made a phone call to General Seminary.

Late one night, I think it was eleven o'clock, a green van pulled up. It says Carolina on the side. It pulls up—there were these guys with boots. They brought up all boots. It was amazing.

One guy jumps out, says, "I heard you need boots." And I told him, "Come on, I'll take you down there." That guy drove from Carolina with boots. I mean, I always abused southerners, and I thought, "Redneck, you're from down south!" But it was incredible. We were one. I brought him down there and he was handing out boots. A fireman gave him one of the hats and he wore it for the two days that he was down there.

*Joanne Ciacciarelli, was the third member of the scheduling team.*

## Joanne Ciacciarelli—This is the best job I ever had.

People were on best behavior. People really wanted to get involved and they really wanted to help. Anybody with bad behavior, anybody who wasn't positive seemed to retreat into the woodwork. We had people who wanted to get in there and help and be part of something that was positive. So I liked to tease Mary, saying, "Mary, this is the best job I ever had." It's best job I've ever had and it's the least amount of money I ever made in my life, because, of course, it was volunteer work.

*The General Theological Seminary's St. Mark's Professor of Ecclesiastical History, the Rev. Dr. J. Robert Wright, observed the activity at the seminary with gratitude. But with an historian's clarity of analysis, he recognized that the tragedy called forth a multiplicity of responses.*

## Bob Wright—God has different roles for each of us.

For me, as a professor at General Seminary, I was profoundly grateful for the swift and informed response that Dean Ward Ewing and so many of our students exhibited in this time of trial. Not since the day that Desmond Tutu was announced here as the winner of the Nobel Prize and the lead anchors of the big three television networks all descended upon us at Chelsea Square, has this place been so galvanized for Christian witness. Our students were busily collecting relief supplies from the stations at the nearby street corners, converting our front lobby into a relief center, organizing additional prayer services in our chapel for crowds of people from off the streets, and, above all, in following the lead of our dean down to the site itself, as volunteers to serve in whatever way they might be helpful.

There is a temptation for all of us to claim some bit of heroism in such a context, but I have to confess that for me, in the face of so many people who seemed to know exactly what ought to be done, I concluded that the role of an activist was not for me. I certainly gave thanks for their witness, but I concluded that I myself could best be of help by just staying out of their way, by continuing my classes on behalf of the others who, for various reasons, chose to stay behind, and by praying and reflecting in my own place rather than rushing to the site of the tragedy. God has different roles for each of us, and we must do what we think we are called to do in the midst of so many sirens and crowds and in the face of such chaos, even as we try also to respect those who discern different directions for their own response.

*In upstate New York, as she watched the television coverage of the recovery effort at the World Trade Center site, Pam Post was baking an apple pie to console a friend whose husband had gone to Manhattan with the National Guard. Looking at the face of one exhausted firefighter, she thought, "How I wish I could send a pie like this to you too." And then she thought, "Why not?" She called a few friends and the Pies from Canandaigua Project was begun.*

## Pam Post—The apple pie, as symbol of the American way of life, seemed important.

I was making an apple pie and the apple pie, as the symbol of the American way of life, suddenly seemed very important. Our whole community was stunned. Everybody was sitting in front of the TV feeling so helpless. All of a sudden, I called a few of my friends, my sister and my sister-in-law about my idea to bake pies for rescue workers at Ground Zero. They liked the idea and liked that it gave us something to do. We even went to the schools and made pies with some of the schoolchildren. All of a sudden we were busy, working with the kids, organizing something. It got our minds off what was happening. It certainly got us away from the television. Getting the community going, getting the kids involved—it was a healthy thing for us. It helped us heal a little bit.

*The women set September 18 as the day to deliver the pies and designated St. Mary's School as the collection site. The Rose Corner Bakery in Canandaigua and Monica's Pies in Naples furnished pie boxes which elementary school children decorated with pictures and messages. J&L Nationaleasing contributed a rental truck; Tom Post used his skill as a cabinetmaker to build interior shelves on which the pies could be stacked. Ewing Lettering and Graphics wrote "Helping Our Heroes" and applied images of apple pies and American flags to the outside panels. Tom recruited two friends, to drive with him to Manhattan with the pies.*

*Tuesday morning an amazing 795 homemade pies were brought to the school, boxed and loaded into the truck and off they went. Tom still wasn't sure where he was going to deliver the pies. Calling the Salvation Army and the Red Cross had produced no one who would accept them, but he had heard that General Theological Seminary was collecting food for the relief effort. When he called there, Mary Morris said, "Yes, we're taking food to the site. Just bring it to the seminary's Ninth Avenue door."*

*The men made the 300-mile drive in record time and arrived just after 7:00 P.M. When Tom entered to say he had some pies for the workers, the student at the desk said, "Just put them there on the ledge." Tom gulped and said, "You don't understand. I have 795 pies." A delivery from GTS was just ready to leave for the Seamen's Church Institute, so Ward Ewing told the pie truck to simply follow him and he'd get the truck into the area. A series of encounters at various roadblocks followed but each time either the smooth-talking dean or the presentation of a pie to the officers at the roadblock opened the way. The Helping Our Heroes truck arrived at Seamen's Church Institute and unloaded about 100 pies for the canteen. From there, escorts appeared as if by magic: a policeman directed the truck to the NYPD emergency headquarters, a national guardsman took the truck to their staging area near Bowling Green Park, and so on. The last pies were left with a line up of ambulances and emergency vehicles along West Street. Tom Post left Manhattan with a panorama of memories imprinted on his mind.*

## Tom Post—There was a lump in my throat the whole time I was there.

I think of the guys coming back to me, saying, "Who sent me this?" "Who are these children who had sent their photographs—this young family here?" And so many policemen and staff there said, "You know, I haven't seen my child in five days." So many of them said that. There was a lump in my throat the whole time I was there. You could smell the burning and the acrid smoke in the air. It was pure emotion. And everyone had it—anyone you ran into—the look in the eyes was shared by everyone. It was like a battlefield situation—guys fully armed, and scared. The soldiers were ready for anything—except an apple pie.

Not everybody at home supported this idea. Half of the people my wife and I talked to beforehand got it and the other half didn't get it. The people who got it were all for it. They couldn't wait. They wanted to do it again and again. They wanted to put notes on the boxes. They knew exactly what the apple pie meant. And the other half of the people said, "Send money." When we met Dean Ewing, he was like Gary Cooper. He was the coolest guy! He was calm, nice, he had a warm smile, and he was a great big tall handsome guy. The first words out of his mouth were positive. "Yeah, we can do that. Great idea! We're going there anyway."

*In the chaos of the early rescue effort, there was little to identify who the pies came from or how they got there. One enterprising EMS worker did find out, and she e-mailed Tom Post.*

## Lt. Lisa Seckler-Roode—This pie quite honestly was the best one I've ever eaten.

Last week, during the worst of the crisis here in New York, one of the lieutenants from my command in the NYC Fire Department EMS Division returned from Ground Zero with food. Included with this food, was an apple pie. On the cover of the box was a hand-drawn American Flag, and on the inside cover, written in hand, was "Thank you so much." Besides the fact that this pie quite honestly was the best one I've ever eaten, the message, as simple as it was, moved all of us greatly. We were all so tired, and so bereft after what we had all experienced working under such terrible circumstances, that IT DID MAKE A DIFFERENCE.

All I can say is, someone from your town made EMS Battalion 45 in Woodside Queens happy in the face of total exhaustion, and sadness. You should be very proud of all your citizens. It warranted letting you know how wonderful it was for us.

# RISING TO THE CHALLENGE
# OF THE NEW REALITY

*By the end of the week, Mark Sisk was inventing new roles for himself and the diocesan staff in the crisis.*

### Mark Sisk—We focused on people who were likely to slip between the cracks.

Very quickly, the diocese became something of a clearinghouse. Usually our work was to point people with resources to other people who were doing a more immediate, more on-the-ground kind of work. And then the further we got from the day, the more our role came to be sort of a funnel by which the concerns of the larger world became focused. We could send resources to particular agencies that were doing things—to St. Paul's or to Episcopal Relief and Development, or to Seamen's Church. Many people generously gave funds that we were able then to distribute.

And we did that in a couple of different ways. We attempted to get funds directly to the people who had been affected by the disaster—the immediate victims. And we focused primarily on those who were likely to slip between the cracks otherwise.

Then another smaller but important part was to focus on those who were providing the direct assistance. We had some chaplains who were working on site almost 24 hours a day, and we gave some support to those people. We also supported people who had particularly difficult work, like the priest who was organizing the chaplains in the Morgue. This is very, very spiritually grinding work, but it is also extraordinarily important work, and we wanted to give some financial resources there. We couldn't really pay people to do that work, but our assistance communicated that what they were doing was something that was supported by the larger community.

*Bishop Sisk also began to mobilize support for the clergy in the diocese, who were the first responders from the church. An early practical suggestion came from the Rt. Rev. Andrew Smith, Bishop of Connecticut, who called to say that one of his parish priests had specialized training in critical incident stress management (CISM). The diocesan staff contacted the Rev. Peter A.R. Stebinger, rector of Christ Church in Bethany. In addition to CISM training, Stebinger had also served as chaplain to the emergency services workers in his town. He held the first CISM workshop for the New York City clergy on the morning of Saturday, September 15 at General Seminary.*

## Peter Stebinger—Our job was to care for the caregivers.

I put a team together—a team of two team leaders plus two peers, usually people trained in stress management. In this case, the peers were clergy. Critical incident stress management, which used to be called debriefing, was designed to deal with a single incident that had ended, like a death in the line of duty, to help people cope with their reactions to an event that was over. No one had ever designed workshops for an incident that wasn't over. So we had to rewrite the book

Bishop Sisk sent out an invitation for the Saturday after 9/11. That morning before the workshops, my team and I had been down to the site, smelled the burning, seen the firefighters working. It was difficult for me to get my team to leave the Trade Center site and go back up to GTS, but our job was to care for the caregiver.

We had about sixty clergy for the two workshops, almost all of whom had seen the towers come down. Some of them were among what I now call the "dust-covered"— people who were so close to the Trade Center that they were covered by those awful clouds of dust. We did what you do in critical incident stress management training. We gave them some tools, and we gave them an opportunity to vent.

We did two different workshops. In each, I started out by saying to them, "What happened on 9/11 was a huge deal, and the fact that you're having a hard time coping with it is not because you're weak. And you need to know that."

And people in the room went, "Oh! We're not crazy, we're not weak, and we don't lack faith. We're in the middle of a huge trauma." I asked everyone in the room to say where they were when the towers came down, and how they were feeling. It was awful. Every single member of my team left the room at some point, because it was too hard to hear it.

What was essential was telling people that it was a huge trauma, that their reactions were normal, and getting them to talk about how they're feeling.

We were trying to help them so they could go straight back to the same terrible place, day after day after day. Among my personal set of heroes are the clergy and lay staff of all the parishes in southern Manhattan. Because I live in Connecticut, I got to go home after it was over. But my friends who were here at Grace Church, at Saint Paul's, at all the churches in Manhattan, they couldn't go home. This was home—where the smoke was, where the Pile was, where the dead were being recovered. And so I came in to give them tools to try to deal with the horror.

*On their own and with guidance from GTS and SCI, volunteers around the city and around the country began to mobilize. The Rev. Chloe Breyer, chaplain at the Cathedral School in New York City, describes the activity there.*

## Chloe Breyer—The children at the Cathedral School.

Children also contributed to the relief effort. One of our eighth graders raised over $1,000 for the Red Cross by setting up a yard sale in his building, and getting other people to join. We had four other seventh or eighth graders who, when we received this incredible trash bag full of teddy bears, went around and delivered them to fire stations for families of firefighters who had died. We had a parent who runs the Chelsea Piers, and offered the Piers up to be a crisis center or a morgue. We must have had children in every grade doing bake sales or raising money for the Red Cross—all really great initiatives.

Then the children wrote cards for not only the firefighters and rescue workers down at Ground Zero, but they also responded to the hundreds of letters that we got from children from around the world who looked us up on the Internet or knew about us for some reason. We got letters from Sydney, Australia, we got letters from London, e-mails from a class in Japan, wanting to interview the kids and find out what they felt. All of these children from around the world drew pictures and sent notes—"We're so sorry, what can we do?" During Evensong, our students wrote thank you notes. We got a huge banner from a community organization in Switzerland, a 20-foot banner that had photographs embroidered into it.

Later the students raised money on Halloween, and their trick-or-treat boxes from UNICEF all went to Afghan children. Our choristers went down to sing at St. Paul's for the rescue workers, which was quite a moving experience for them.

*Once the dispirited staff at Trinity Wall Street realized that their offices were going to be closed for some time, they began to look for other office space. Trinity's endowment, or "patrimony," includes ownership of nearly six million feet of office space in Manhattan. Within a few days, space was found in one of these buildings, and the staff moved in and began to grapple with the painful memories of the events that had happened only three blocks from their offices on Trinity Place. The Rev. Dr. Daniel Paul Matthews, rector of Trinity Church, described the relocation.*

## Dan Matthews—Trinity finds temporary office space.

It wasn't very long after the attacks that we realized we had to try to put things back together. And what did that mean? Where would we go? How would we start afresh? Everything we had was in the Trinity Place building that was blocked off. How could we get back in the building to get the materials we needed?

Getting back to work seemed to be a very important emotional, spiritual, and psychological challenge. To be able to get back to doing what we were supposed to do gave us a renewed sense that maybe we'd make it, maybe there was a future, maybe there was some hope. But until we could do our work again, it felt like there was no light at the end of the tunnel. Work and a place and a desk and a structured re-entry into the challenges of doing my job were for me a critical element of healing.

After a few days, we reconvened at one of our empty spaces at 100 Sixth Avenue. Not only could we get back to our work, but we could talk to each other. And boy, did we do that! We needed to say, "Where were you? What did you do?" and then we'd say it the next day. "And what did your mother think?" "Let me tell you about my mother. Oh my goodness, my mother was . . ." "Well tell me about your brother." "Oh my brother..." and then there was a long story. All of those stories kind of needed to be, and were, slowly told in the context of the work environment. Contrast that with a situation where you've just had a disaster and everybody scatters and doesn't re-gather. The re-gathering becomes a way of spiritually important healing and reconnecting. If you're all right, then maybe I'm all right. And if I can tell you I'm all right, then maybe I can hear that you're alright. So the coming together in the workplace, for me, began to kind of create the tribe again, the community again, the family again.

And here's another factor. It was a big floor, big enough that everybody's office was on one floor, and when you walked out of your office, you walked by all of these open cubicles, and that created even more community. In our building on Trinity Place, you have to ride the elevator to see somebody, because we are spread out on nine or ten floors. At our temporary quarters, we had community automatically. Everybody got off of the same elevator. Everybody bumped into each other at the coffee machine. You went in there, there were three or four people making coffee.

Then we brought the therapists in, and they had an office there. You could walk by and stick your head in and say hi and do your therapy in a few minutes. Or you could sit down and say, "Could I have an hour sometime tomorrow?" There were also formal occasions for people to tell their stories. We got groups together, around a table, and each person talked about his or her experiences.

We didn't want to force people into a therapeutic model. It was okay if they said, "I'm not ready to talk." And some people were far less ready to talk immediately than they were a month later. I found these groups extremely powerful. People, for example, who were usually very articulate and verbose often clammed up and couldn't talk. And some of the people who had never said a word told incredible stories, like walking across the Brooklyn Bridge and all the way home. One woman said, "I got home, and my mother hugged me, and we cried, and she asked me, 'Where are your shoes?'" She looked down and she said, "Shoes? I don't know." She'd walked six miles into Brooklyn without her shoes, and didn't even know it.

*All through the week, churches opened their doors for quiet prayers and added extra services. Chloe Breyer recalls the service at the cathedral on Friday.*

### Chloe Breyer—Worship services continue at the Cathedral of St. John the Divine

On September 14, the national day of prayer, the cathedral was packed for the Friday service. It was also Holy Cross Day. Storm Swain, who is a priest on staff here, suggested that instead of doing a sermon, we anoint people. That was exactly what people wanted and needed. It was amazing because it enabled the personal contact that everyone was looking for. Jay Wegman, the cathedral's Canon for Liturgy, organized it. We just did it. He pulled priests out of a hat, I don't know where he found everybody. But there were enough priests and we set up anointing stations throughout the cathedral. In the midst of the service, everyone who wanted was anointed with oil in the sign of the cross. And people really responded to that.

*Others who attended that service remember worshipers weeping in the arms of the priests as they came forward to be anointed. Later that night, the cathedral held another service. The Most Rev. Frank Griswold, Presiding Bishop of the Episcopal Church in the United States, attended.*

## Frank Griswold—Carrying the light of hope into the darkness.

On the Friday after the 9/11, I went to the Cathedral of St. John the Divine for an impromptu service at the end of the day for which several thousand people showed up. And at the end of the service, the people who were in the congregation were given candles and asked to take the candles out onto the vast steps of the cathedral and then from there to disperse into the city carrying the light of hope into the darkness of all that had happened to us.

Mark Sisk, the Bishop of New York, and I led the congregation out with our candles. People gathered on the steps. And no one dispersed.

I said to Mark, "Why don't we go down the steps. Maybe if we go down to the sidewalk, this will be the cue that people are to go their several ways." So we went down to the base of the steps. No one moved. In fact, people passing by inquired about what was going on and joined the people on the steps. Some even went off and brought candles of their own so that they could participate fully. Finally we began to sing songs like "We Shall Overcome," and I had a sense that what people needed more than anything else was simply to be together.

# OFFICIAL CEREMONIES AT GROUND ZERO AND YANKEE STADIUM

*Soon after the attacks, New York City officials invited religious leaders to help plan for ceremonies to honor the dead and console their families and friends. Together with other key religious leaders, Bishop Sisk and Archdeacon Kendall met with Mayor Giuliani at the emergency command center. The Mayor's initial concern was funerals for the thousands who had died, but attention soon turned to President Bush's planned visit on Friday, September 14, and discussion of the best site for a huge memorial service the next weekend. Cardinal John Egan offered St. Patrick's, the Roman Catholic Cathedral, Mark Sisk suggested the Cathedral of St. John the Divine, but the Mayor chose Yankee Stadium.*

*During the President's visit on Friday, the religious leaders had little role to play, but at the Yankee Stadium service on Sunday, September 23, their role was central. Christians, Muslims and Jews all participated. In the Protestant segment, the Rev. Calvin Butts, pastor of the Abyssinian Baptist Church in Harlem, was the primary speaker. In an electric moment, he reached out to those present, saying,*

This memorial service is for you, and I hope that at this time you will take the hands of the person who sits on either side of you. You may know them, you may not; but if we are going to stand in unity, we have to at least unify by the joining of our hands and hearts. I want you to turn to your neighbor and say, "We are going to get through this. We are going to get through this."

*Bishop Sisk followed with a short prayer.*

Almighty God, be with us and comfort us in this tragic hour.

Give us the assurance of your presence.

Strengthen and heal the brokenhearted who must face the future
   deprived of the companionship of those closest to them.

Guide the President and leaders of the world.

Let justice be done.

Let the poor and destitute be lifted up.

Let peace prevail.

We give thanks for this great land and the ideals that it stands for.

We give thanks to you for the grace, courage and sacrifice of so many.

Drive from our hearts all hate and prejudice.

   Amen.

# 3

## ST. PAUL'S CHAPEL

*St. Paul's Chapel is five blocks north of Trinity Church. Established by Trinity in 1766 as a "chapel of ease," a chapel for those living beyond a convenient walking distance to the church, in 2001 it stood on the block west of the World Trade Center. Shortly before the towers fell, St. Paul's had begun to revitalize its neighborhood ministry. There was no parish hall, no office space, but it was beautiful and elegant and graceful—a small architectural jewel with seating for about 250 worshipers, the oldest continuously used public building in New York City. George Washington had gone to pray at St. Paul's Chapel immediately after his inauguration as president, April 30, 1789. The chapel contains one of the earliest representations of the Great Seal of the United States, a painting that has hung over the presidential pew in the chapel since 1789. This small church had been a repository of treasured memories and artifacts at the heart of American history.*

*The fortunes of St. Paul's waxed and waned just as the fashion and demography of its city did. During the Civil War the size of the congregation rivaled the old mother Trinity Church on Wall Street, but by 2001 the flock had dwindled. In March 2001 the rector of Trinity named the Rev. Lyndon Harris, a doctoral student from General Theological Seminary, who had served parishes in New York City and South Carolina, as associate for St. Paul's Chapel. His mission was to reach out to the growing residential population of the neighborhood, making use of alternative forms of worship and experimental music and media. His dream was that St. Paul's would become a "laboratory of urban evangelism and alternative worship." By high summer of 2001, St. Paul's was occasionally drawing up to 200 worshipers to hip-hop masses and jazz liturgies. Then the pendulum swung and this historic little church moved once more to the center of American history.*

# SEPTEMBER 12

### Lyndon Harris—St. Paul's Chapel has survived.

On September 12 I walked down Broadway from my apartment in Greenwich Village, a mile and a half away. I was assuming that St. Paul's was demolished. How could it have survived? As I got just about to City Hall, three blocks up the street, there was a clearing between the buildings and I could see the spire of St. Paul's Chapel standing proud. I could not believe it. And to walk into this place the first time after the attack of 9/11 was an extraordinary experience. The place so eerie, yet so filled with spiritual energy, was covered with soot, but it was almost as if sparks were flying off my boots as I walked in. It was clear to me that we were spared, not because we were holier than anybody who died across the street, but because we had a big job to do.

I didn't stay very long because I didn't know if the structure was safe. I'll never forget leaving, going outside, and there I encountered a firefighter who asked if he could come inside the chapel and sleep. He had been working for almost twenty-four hours. And I told him he couldn't because I didn't know that the chapel was safe. I'll never forget the look on his face. It haunted me until we got things open and going at St. Paul's. His haggard face is etched in my memory.

### Tim O'Neill of the New York Police Department—The chapel was saved for a purpose.

The day after the attack I was looking around for a bathroom. I saw footprints going into St. Paul's, and I thought, "Oh, it must be open." So I opened the door, and I walked inside. It was pitch dark, eerily silent. Every part of the chapel was covered with about six inches of dust. The dust was yellow with a sort of white powder mixed in with it. I had my flashlight and I made my way to the bathroom in the back. I used the restroom, then walked out and started looking around the church. I thought, "Look at that, not even a window is broken in here. I can't believe that, because right behind the graveyard it's the towers, the rubble wasn't thirty feet away." I saw George Washington's box, I got a little information about it, what St. Paul's was. I said, "Wow that's unbelievable." It had a little spirituality and a little reminder; to me at least, it was protected. It was immediately designated as a sanctuary by a higher power, which was great. Unbelievable.

# SEPTEMBER 13–15

*By Wednesday September 13, Lyndon Harris was attempting to maintain a pastoral presence at St. Paul's. By Friday morning September 14, he was joined by the Rev. Lloyd Prator, rector of Saint John's in the Village. They talked and prayed with rescue workers, gave blessings, and heard confessions.*

*Each day more and more rescuers, firefighters, and policemen stopped by to rest, use the bathrooms, and wash up. The chapel was still lit only by candles and flashlights. St. Paul's had survived, but the building and churchyard were covered in inches of dust and papers. The digging out from the debris began on September 13. It took several days to clean out the cemetery, even though one set of Venetian blinds from the Twin Towers remained hanging in the cemetery trees for weeks.*

*President Bush proclaimed September 14 a national day of prayer and asked that all church bells be rung at noon. The rector requested that the bell be rung. Trinity building manager Mike Borrero and director of Trinity Property Management Jim Doran and Lyndon Harris ran to the chapel, as requested by the rector, to see if the bell at St. Paul's could be rung. They climbed the dark bell tower at 11:30 that day.*

## Jim Doran—The bells of St. Paul's ring out once again.

We went back into the church, and we decided to go up and see if we could get into the bell tower. On the way up Mike Borrero found a piece of plumbing. We climbed up to the top of the bell tower and I held a flashlight on the bell. And I believe the date on the bell is 1797. Lyndon told us by his watch that it was noon. Then Mike Borrero took the pipe and hit the bell twelve times, or as he has been quoted as saying, "I beat the hell out of that bell." And when that bell rang out all the policemen and the firemen took their hats off and turned around and faced the church because they had no idea that anyone was in the church nor that the bell could possibly be rung.

*Inspectors had not yet given the official green light to open St. Paul's for permanent occupancy. By Friday night, September 14 pressure was being put on Lyndon Harris to let people come into the chapel on a regular basis.*

## Lyndon Harris–I got into a brouhaha with an actress.

The pressure was mounting on me to open the chapel up. On Friday night I got into a brouhaha with the actress Juliana Margulies, who used to be one of the stars of the television show *ER*. She was hell-bent on coming into St. Paul's and I was hell-bent on keeping her out. I did not know that the building was safe and I did not want it collapsing on people. It was a good-natured brouhaha. Margulies had courageously opened a food service close by and was doing outstanding service to the workers, and she wanted to be able to come into St. Paul's to sit. I said, "I'd love to do that, but I'm not sure the building is safe." Margulies said, "How do we find out if it's safe?" I said, "I have to get a structural engineer in here to check it out." She said, "Well, I'll get you one." But I said that, since I worked for Trinity, we needed someone that Trinity, the institution, could certify. Finally the Police Department structural engineer checked it out and gave us the go-ahead.

*It still took a few days for St. Paul's to become fully open. In the meantime providing meals for rescue workers had begun right on Broadway, in front of the chapel. By September 15 volunteers from Seamen's Church Institute and Grace Church were cooking hamburgers and hot dogs using first a grill from St. Paul's shelter and later welding together huge grills to keep up with the volume of food demanded. This cooking operation would continue around the clock into the next week. Volunteers began to deliver water and supplies to rescue workers out on the Pile of Ground Zero. The Rev. James L. Burns and the Rev. Thomas H. Synan, Episcopal priests from the Church of the*

*Heavenly Rest on the Upper East Side of Manhattan, now joined Lyndon Harris. The primitive relief effort of St. Paul's Chapel at Ground Zero had now begun.*

# THE NATURE OF THE WORK AT GROUND ZERO

*To understand the ministry of St. Paul's Chapel it is necessary to know about the hard reality of the work at Ground Zero, which would last until May 23, 2002. There were two tasks in these nine months. The first was the recovery and identification of the remains of the dead. Ultimately 1,300 bodies were found in part or in whole. Second, the ruins of the seven buildings of the World Trade Center had to be dismantled and carted away.*

*This task was performed not by volunteers, but by unionized workers—firefighters, police, sanitation workers, constructions workers, carpenters, and EMS workers—a total force of 5,000 men and women committed to the effort.*

*These professionals generally worked in twelve-hour shifts for one-month tours of duty. As they worked their way through the debris, there were changes in the terrain of Ground Zero. As more concrete, steel, and ash were removed, the Pile became the Pit. But there were constants throughout the nine months. From first to last the work was grim, dangerous, and exhausting, taxing to mind, body, and spirit. Surrounding the physical enterprise of Ground Zero was the emotional tide of the grieving relatives of the lost and pilgrims from all over the world who began to swarm to the site, as if at a holy place. Some of the workers could not withstand the stress and left. Thousands stayed for the nine months, contributing more of themselves, not less.*

*The ministry of St. Paul's Chapel was dedicated to these thousands of volunteer and professional workers at the sixteen acres of devastated ruin in Lower Manhattan.*

*For the first weeks after 9/11 the ministry of St. Paul's was crucial for four reasons:*

1. *Provision of food—There were very few restaurants or grocery stores open in Manhattan below Canal Street.*

2.  *Care of feet—Fires burned continuously under the Pit for weeks and the workers needed treatment for blistered feet and burned out boots. Melted boots had to be replaced.*

3.  *The horrific nature of the work—The state of the bodies recovered was described variously as "bags of jelly" or "decapitated gray stuff wrapped around bones."*

4.  *Rest—There was no other place available for workers easily to lie down, clean up, and catch a few hours of sleep. So the workers began to wander into St. Paul's and sleep on the hard wooden pews.*

*The Rev. Larry Provenzano is rector of St. Andrew's Church, Longmeadow, Massachusetts, and a fire department chaplain. He was one of the early rescue workers who arrived from out of state.*

## Larry Provenzano—The scene is beyond human comprehension in its magnitude.

The scene is beyond human comprehension in its magnitude and assault on the senses. In its shadow we work to minister to the needs of firefighters and rescue workers, praying over human remains collected in body bags, and attempting to offer comfort to the colleagues and families of the missing and dead.

My heart aches, my body hurts, my soul is touched by the tremendous pain of God's people in this place. I think to myself, this must be what hell is like. Yet this is a holy place, a holy time, redeemed by the presence of God's people—the human family doing the possible in an impossible situation.

People have said nothing will ever be the same—I believe that may be true. We never should be the same—not after this. We should grow in our understanding that God is in the midst of us, even in the darkest time of our living. We should develop a deeper appreciation for our calling to sacrifice, to give unconditionally, and to love our brothers and sisters with the love of God that is in us.

Hatred brought forth this time in our lives—love will conquer it. I am not sure why God has put me here—all I know is that at this moment I am the church, dressed in the turn out gear and helmet of my fire department, carrying with me the healing presence of the Christ I love and serve in the people around me at Ground Zero.

# SCI OPENS A ST. PAUL'S FEEDING STATION

*The Seamen's Church Institute, created in 1834 as an outreach ministry of the Episcopal Church to seafarers and the most durable of the many organizations founded in the nine-teenth century to promote seamen's welfare, is located seven blocks east of St. Paul's, on Water Street at the end of Fulton Street. With its location and long-standing experience of outreach in times of disaster, SCI became the first staging area for Episcopal relief in Lower Manhattan. SCI's emergency relief operations for workers began on the afternoon of 9/11 and continued for twelve days. By September 13, SCI was bringing supplies to Ground Zero and by September 15, SCI had opened feeding operations in front of St. Paul's Chapel. The executive director of the Institute was Peter Larom.*

## Peter Larom—The church is a great sleeping giant.

Finally, on the Saturday following 9/11 we realized that the front porch of St. Paul's would be an ideal place to set up a canteen. So we were working on getting all of our food and our grills out on that porch at the other end of Fulton Street, only a few blocks away. It was a logistical effort getting all of this stuff down Fulton Street, through the roadblocks, and getting set up.

Watching the churches and people respond without meetings, without strategic plans, simply the church moving into action emphasized for me that the church is a great sleeping giant, with huge spiritual and physical resources, with buildings and people and skills and resources. September 11 called that forth. We were able to see the church that day in action in a way that demonstrated its power.

*The relief operation at SCI continued until September 23. Then the remaining supplies were transferred to St. Paul's so that SCI could return to its primary focus, the ministry to seafarers. Karen Sisk, wife of the Bishop of New York, joined the volunteers.*

## Karen Sisk—All day we were stuffing hamburgers and hotdogs into buns.

On the morning of September 17 I rode over to St. Paul's from the Seamen's Church Institute in a truck. There were an enormous number of people around the food stations. There were uniformed officers and firefighters, police and construction workers, so many people down there working. There were very few slow moments. I must have been down there six or seven hours, stuffing hamburgers and hotdogs into buns and giving them to people. All day hamburgers and hotdogs were cooking on several grills. Trucks kept bringing in food.

And then a couple of people, just a few people, started to go inside the chapel just to sit. Then someone lay out on the pew to try to sleep. More people filed in, just to sit or sleep, because in contrast to all the noise outside the church, it was very quiet inside. And still, while people tried to sleep in this stillness, there was powdery dust all over everything.

By September 17 they had already set up a coffee and food station inside the church on the left hand side. There were several tables in a row, lined up length-wise with coffee and food and that kind of thing. Actually the place was an absolute mess. We said, "Well, the least we can do is clean this up, make some order out of this." So we did that. We set about cleaning up the place because coffee had spilled and sugar was all over. We cleaned up for awhile and then we went back outside.

I am very glad I went down to help. It was time out of time. When I try to think back on it now, I was so struck by how hard everyone was working and everyone was pulling together to make things happen. Just the little vignettes, like someone would walk by completely covered with a zoot suit, literally with even the booties over their shoes. It was an amazing array of people. The FBI would come by and I knew they were FBI because they had FBI in great big letters on the back of their jackets. I was impressed with how many women I saw in those roles. The majority were men, but I noticed that there were women. The quietness of the church—the activity outside and then the stillness inside of the church was very dramatic to me. Whenever I went in and out of there,

I could see people sitting with very vacant expressions on their faces. They could rest in there and get away from it just a little bit.

### Frank Griswold—It was as though you had Mary and Martha.

In the course of these days it was as though you had Mary and Martha. The active Martha was represented by the Seamen's Church Institute, and the contemplative silent Mary was represented by St. Paul's Chapel. Both elements are so important. The church needs to be actively present in direct service. But the church also needs to provide space, silence, where people can simply be alone with whatever they are living and experiencing, and the mystery of God. I thought, "Isn't this wonderful that we have both dimensions represented here in the midst of all that is going on." And how important those two dimensions are always to have some creative tension with one another.

# SEPTEMBER 17–20

*For the next five days St. Paul's functioned as a makeshift and informal haven for emergency crews and anyone else in need during those first terrible days. Scores of volunteers recruited from the temporary communications center at the General Theological Seminary, coordinated the still-informal ministry. They struggled to provide hundreds of hungry, tired workers with everything from food and drink to eye drops, clean underwear and a quiet place to catch a little sleep. These days have been characterized as movement from chaos to the first structured ministry of relief.*

### Lyndon Harris—Chaos.

From September 17 on people started coming into St. Paul's. I knew the building was safe and I did not have any qualms about people coming in. A few clergy started arriving to help me like Jim Burns from Heavenly Rest and Tom Synan, who is his assistant, and Tom soon had the nickname "Tom Heaven." They were down here early. And we had a lot of strange people, looking to get involved in some way. In fact one of the biggest jobs, early on, was to weed out the crazies.

When I hear people say, "Oh, St. Paul's just happened," I think, "Hell no, this didn't just happen." It just about killed me, because I was there all the time to manage this thing. It was out of control. I was trying to keep people safe. I had the restoration people from Sotheby's take out and store the paintings and the Great Seal of the United States and the Chippendale chairs.

General Seminary was around from the very beginning. One of the first shifts of volunteers to come to St. Paul's came from the seminary. During those first days my greatest mission was simply to be a clearinghouse to decide amidst this chaotic atmosphere what ministries we wanted to empower and support. We decided not to do a medical/surgical operation. We decided not to have a barber, or clown ministries, but by the first Sunday we decided that we did want to have a daily Eucharist at noon.

Protocol was out the door—this was a combat zone. You still have to have some protocol, of course, but it is not high on the list. There are reasonably sane individuals and there are, in a situation like this, less-than-sane individuals. We had a guy coming in as a podiatrist's assistant with a collar on. He was a Roman Catholic clergy person—so he said—dispensing the sacraments, when he was supposed to be working on people's feet. So I had to ask him to leave. Some guys showed up from conservative television ministries and they were filming. They had a little camera in a Twinkies box and they were going around handing out Twinkies and filming at the same time. They were sending the film back to their television studio. I said, "We don't want you to do this here. Do it in the street if you like but leave us alone."

### Fred Burnham—It was a perfect model of a free, open and evolving organism.

By Wednesday, September 19 volunteers were grilling hundreds of hamburgers at a time. The crowds were pretty big. I was the Trinity representative that night, and there were some volunteers from General Seminary and Seamen's Church Institute. What transpired that night was really fascinating. I began to realize that this night was exemplary, that in crises like this, people come together spontaneously and teams of people emerge to meet certain crises. And what you get is a perfect model of a free, open, and evolving organism. In chaos and complexity theory it is called self-organizing systems. St. Paul's was on the verge that night of using new solutions of organization to solve critical problems, but what happened that night was really comic because roles got reversed.

The Health Department showed up and they decided that they were going to shut us down. This team arrived and started taking the hamburgers off the grills and pouring lye on them. But the policemen loved their barbecue on Broadway. The first thing I knew, this team of five people from the Health Department was surrounded by cops. They marched them off the premises and said, "Don't come back!"

A second health team was sent, all male. And the next thing I knew the cops and the Health Department team were standing on the steps of St. Paul's shoving one another. I thought I was going to have to break up a fight, but the cops prevailed again. An hour later a third team from the State Department of Health arrived with a written order from Mayor Giuliani that said, "Shut it down." And the cops stood at attention, because Rudy was their hero and whatever Rudy said, went. So they shut us down. This was about midnight, but the food service was up and going the next day—all again, this self-organizing system of spontaneous generation.

What had happened was that Courtney Cowart, a recent doctoral graduate from General Seminary and a grants officer at Trinity Church, had witnessed this entire scene. She called her cousin Martin Cowart, whose restaurant on Vesey Street had recently closed down. Martin knew all the Health Department officials but he didn't know what to do with the rest of his life. So on Thursday morning Courtney called and said, "Martin, I think we have a new vocation for you."

# SEPTEMBER 20–22

*By Saturday, September 22, Labor of Love, a national relief effort based in Ashville, North Carolina, spearheaded by Bethany Anne Putnam, had arrived at St. Paul's, adding much needed structure to the ministry. Bethany Putnam had been working in relief ministries for about three years. Her primary contact at Trinity Church was Courtney*

*Cowart, the Trinity grants officer and scholar of Anglican spirituality. Putnam brought on board as her assistant, Katherine Avery of South Carolina. Lyndon Harris had been Katherine Avery's youth minister nine years earlier. Courtney enlisted her cousin Martin to be in charge of food. So two weeks after 9/11, St. Paul's had a staff made up of Lyndon Harris, Amy Boldosser, Bethany Putnam, Courtney Cowart, Katherine Avery, and Martin Cowart, all with some previous personal links that molded them quickly into a team.*

### Courtney Cowart–I've got two ideas.

On the morning after the Health Department had tried to shut us down I said to Lyndon, "I've got two ideas. One I'd like to call this woman Bethany Putnam in North Carolina, because this is exactly her thing. And secondly, I'd like to call my cousin Martin whose restaurant has closed, but he knows the Health Department officials, and he has a certified food license." Martin arrived the next day, and Bethany loaded up her trailer and was in operation by Saturday with her assistant, Katherine Avery, whom she had just hired the Friday before. It sort of happened spontaneously in the moment, and everything took on a life of its own, but now Katherine, Bethany, Martin, Lyndon, and I were all in the chapel together.

Lyndon was really chief pastor. Bethany Putnam was the person who had the vision of what St. Paul's became: chiropractors, podiatrists, massage therapists. She would sit up in the gallery and watch everything, and her goal was to think of everything that workers really needed. Katherine Avery had responsibility for volunteers, interfacing with Mary Morris and General Seminary. Martin masterminded the food operation. I was the administrative person. We had a staff meeting each morning, and I spent the rest of the day attempting to solve the problems that had been identified.

The focus of St. Paul's was service, simple acts of human kindness, that were spontaneously generated by people who wanted to give something, who wanted to do something, anything, and were given the freedom to think of a creative way of expressing that—expressing simple acts of human kindness to one another.

St. Paul's was a space that allowed acts of kindness to take place. It overflowed with every kind of religious symbolism, every kind of denominational allegiance or identity. It was radically multi-faith. I always thought that the architecture of St. Paul's was a happy accident because there was at first such a minimal amount of imaging, that it could be filled up and express the ministry as it evolved.

## Martin Cowart—We were able to channel funds back into the local economy.

We had no kitchen, no storage facility, and no electricity. And we had to get the food through the barricades. And they wanted hot food. So I contracted with various catering companies like Mary Cleaver and La Zie. At first I was trying to keep it to a limited number because to get something through the three police barricades was a task—to get three hundred hot meals in here and served while they were hot was a logistical nightmare when we had no power.

In the beginning I worked with Mary Cleaver and La Zie for our evening meals and for lunch I worked with Zabar's. And what that allowed me to do is to pass through to our local economy the funds that were coming in for the relief operations from all over the world. Before it was all over, I had an almost $1,000,000 budget that I was able to channel back into the local economy through these various distributors and catering companies and local restaurants. These people were hurting because the restaurant industry was in such a shambles after 9/11. It had that trickle-down effect because if the restaurants were not doing well, they were not buying food from the distributors, who then weren't buying food from the farmers. I think that was an important part of the relief effort to our community.

And then eventually as the barriers came down, and access to Lower Manhattan was less restricted I began to contract with more local restaurants. They were so appreciative. I mean, there's Edwards, Le Zinc, Michael's on Broadway, El Teddy's, H. & H. Bagels, Krispy Kreme Donuts, Dunkin' Donuts, Café Seaport—that was huge. Café Seaport lost two restaurants in the World Trade Center. They were so appreciative. They would deliver forty quarts of soup a day—at really unbelievably low prices.

## Katherine Avery—You can't help but want to be here.

Our main job when Labor of Love arrived was to get everything organized, put everything in its place, find beds, find blankets, pillows, everything that people needed, all this to get us where we could really function as a rescue center. It's incredible what has transpired here: podiatrists, chiropractors, massage therapists, food from gourmet restaurants in New York City, supplies, services, procedures all in place so that we could really help people. By the time the ministry was set up, you could not but be changed when you came into this place: smiles, hugs, letters, donations, pictures, anything that people can give. When you are surrounded by that twenty-four hours a day, it is hard not to be changed. You can't help but want to be here.

## Bethany Putnam—St. Paul's was all about ultimate hospitality.

The phrase I've used over and over again about what St. Paul's was all about is "ultimate hospitality." I felt that we were there, and my role was to make sure that the rescue workers were being taken care of to the best of our ability. They were so tired and they had so much on their minds that we had to think of every last need that they had and offer it to them before they realized they needed it. That they had personal contact with somebody who was really looking out for them, that was really the most important part of it, that is what "ultimate hospitality" was all about.

But also my real second commitment was to the volunteers who were coming in. I felt it was so important that this be a site where civilian volunteers could come in and the parishes could have an opportunity to do group building: to be a part of an experience like this and then to go back to their own towns, homes, neighbors, churches and really talk about the experience. I was proud that the chapel was able to stay open as long as it did, and that it was a place where people could come and really be a part of the experience.

In the end I was at St. Paul's for about five weeks. I got there on September 21 and I was there until just before Halloween. I was there for the whole month of October and the last half of September. When I left there I was worn out, I don't think I made it past the Pocono's. Went into a hotel and I think I slept for about 14 hours.

# OCTOBER 31–JUNE 2

*In the first weeks of November St. Paul's fell into the pattern that would remain in place until the operations at Ground Zero came to an end in May 2002, and the St. Paul's relief effort ended on June 2. There were staff changes: Sr. Grace, a novice of the Society of St. Margaret, arrived to serve with Courtney Cowart and to regularize the administration of the operation. Diane Reiners, a New Yorker and a member of the congregation of the Cathedral of Saint John the Divine with experience as a cook and as a supervisor in catering operations, was brought in to schedule volunteers and to work with Katherine Avery. From November on Dennis Fisin and Carter Booth greeted and trained volunteers and performed a variety of tasks in the chapel.*

*The quality of relief matured over time. The grilled hamburgers and hot dogs were replaced by gourmet fare from Bouley's Bakery and the Waldorf Astoria. Long tables were piled high with fresh fruit, bananas, apples, oranges, candy, cookies, power bars, gum, and cigarettes. Like Ground Zero, St. Paul's was open 24/7, volunteers from the region and from across the country streamed in to serve from 1,500 to 3,000 meals a day during two twelve-hour shifts, handing out 250,000 tubes of chap stick, providing grief counseling, prayer, music, church services, solace, medical attention, support, changing the linen daily on the cots that lined the walls of the ground floor of the sanctuary and the gallery. The chapel became a place where workers could get in touch with God and with their fellow human beings, through the ministries of listening, touch, and tenderness.*

*Though no one on the team, when interviewed, claimed ownership of particular policies or ideas, they all agreed that a basic pattern of operation had emerged by November. A clear organizational pattern was set up: there was a daily morning meeting of the permanent team. Volunteers would serve in teams of twelve for twelve-hour shifts. Churches or other organizations were asked to provide an entire team, if possible with a designated captain, through whom arrangements would be finalized. Scheduling of volunteers would be handled on site at St. Paul's. There was a clear administrative structure, but also regular staff consultation to catch small problems before they became enormous. Two ideas dominated everything: "empowering the volunteers" and "radical hospitality," the practice of daily, ordinary loving of all the Ground Zero workers who came into the chapel.*

**Sister Grace—We wanted to be a community of Christian hope and healing.**

At St. Paul's Chapel we wanted to be a community of Christian hope and healing for all engaged in the work at Ground Zero. We saw our ministry as providing an oasis of hospitality, service and pastoral care during this time of crisis and grief. We encouraged gifts to be offered and accepted in this place: services of people present, but also gifts of those who were not able to be physically present but could offer prayer, money, supplies.

In reality we were a chaotic hotel of radical hospitality, chaotic because we were serving up to 1,500 people and more each day coming through our doors. We had everything from anthrax scares to days in which we completely ran out of supplies and had to scrounge for stuff we needed. On other days we were simply overwhelmed by the generosity: cards, letters, donations, from everywhere—Japan, Germany, Oklahoma, Alabama—that generosity was at times chaotic too.

Eventually, as things settled into a pattern, I was the pastoral coordinator. I was in charge of making sure we had clergy twenty-four hours a day, seven days a week. So I was on the phone all the time. Anyone looking for me was told, "Look for the nun with the cell phone." I was finding, recruiting, and scheduling clergy. We had three shifts a day for clergy and two shifts a day for laity. I was essentially the clergy police, screening out people without ID's, checking out strange priests or nuns who suddenly appeared at our door, you know like the Missionaries of Charity, Mother Theresa's nuns, a whole group of them showed up at our door, and the word was —"Go get Sr. Grace, the clergy police."

**Diane Reiners—Katherine and I handled the lay volunteers.**

Katherine Avery and I were parallel to Sr. Grace in that she handled the clergy and we handled the lay volunteers. Katherine and I got close to 60 calls a day from people wanting to volunteer. We were the ultimate velvet rope. There were not enough volunteer slots for all the people who wanted to volunteer. We gave the volunteers their orientation, we handed out the jobs, we sent them on their way, and in about ten minutes someone always would come back to me and ask if we had any more Chap Stick. And my job was to say where it was, upstairs, on the left.

In the end I think we had something like over 10,000 volunteers in here. We have had something in the vicinity of over half a million visits. No wonder the marble of Saint Paul's is not as shiny as it once was.

What was our mission? It was pastoral care. And I believe that the pastoral care we did here is much more effective than the usual crisis counseling. People needed somebody to say, "I'm here for you," and they needed somebody's shoulder to cry on. The atmosphere of St. Paul's conditioned people to open up in this way. It was the community. It was the space. Both said: "I'm always available, I can always give you follow-ups, I want to be there wherever you end up."

## Martin Cowart—Rescue workers like good food.

I've handled the food service operation here because that is my background. I've served hundreds of thousands of meals at St. Paul's, and food in this ministry was the main nutrient. It was one of the main sources of comfort. A lot of people who were working on this site probably would not have come into this church if it were not for the opportunity to have a meal. And rescue workers like good food. They don't really want cold cuts, or sandwiches, or rations. They want food that is hot, whether it's a hot meal, or hot soup, or in the morning, oatmeal or grits.

What has serving this good food meant to me? It has been the most transforming experience I've ever had in my life, for certain. St. Paul's has made everything in the world come to a sense of reality for me: to see human beings interact with one another with such tremendous amounts of love, compassion and spirituality. When you actually experience this type of interaction with human beings, in this degree, there is a new spiritual reality that springs up in our lives, that you can clearly see. Serving food at St. Paul's gave me a real sense of clarity in my purpose of living. That is the most important thing that has happened to me in these past nine months.

## Carter Booth—We also have beds along the sides here at St. Paul's.

We also have beds along the sides here at St. Paul's. Beds are a very important component of the spiritual services that we offer. I don't think there was any place in Manhattan after the first month following 9/11 that you could really walk into and take a nap and nobody would disturb you. People may have had trouble sleeping, but they felt comfortable sleeping here. People come in to sleep here for all kinds of different reasons. If the men on the Pile work twelve hours, have an hour's drive home and then have to leave an hour early to get here, they basically don't have much time left in their days. If they have a break during the day, they'll come in here and take a nap. So providing a place to sleep opens up communication.

### Lyndon Harris—I was a coach encouraging the team to do their best.

What was my role at St. Paul's? I was a coach in a sense, encouraging the team to do what they could do best. I was the coach who had to empower the team, and I was the coach who played defense with the institution. I found that I had to be there almost every waking moment because decisions had to be made from one moment to another. The experience was an extraordinary invitation to me to work on my improvisational skills. We had to improvise as we went.

We tried to set up an environment at St. Paul's that accepted and empowered the gifts of others. I think that was the unique thing about the ministry that made it successful— messy, organic, seeming to be disorganized, but one of the great gifts was that we accepted the gifts of others. We gave them freedom to offer their gifts and it was always interesting to see how different groups would respond to the invitation.

What I tried to offer at St. Paul's was an integrated approach to ministry where all the needs of the human being were taken into consideration, especially the needs of the body. For the people who were having their boots burned off, we had podiatrists. For those who had sore muscles, we had massage therapists. For those whose bones were not working any more, we had chiropractors.

I think wholeness is very much at the heart of holiness, and that is one reason why we were so influential in the relief effort—because we were able to embrace that, and I think our theology enabled us to embrace that. One of the ways I have described the work I was doing at St. Paul's, the alternative worship I was doing, is "multi-sensory rhetoric." It is worship and ministry that appeals to all of the senses, treats all of the senses. Using different kinds of music and lighting and visual stuff took on a whole new meaning in the relief operation that was St. Paul's.

# WORSHIP AT ST. PAUL'S

*From September 16 through June 2 the Eucharist was celebrated each noon at the altar of St. Paul's Chapel according to the liturgy of the Episcopal Church in the Book of Common Prayer. There were also many special services in the chapel: Thanksgiving, Christmas, Ash Wednesday, the Easter Vigil, the service that marked the closing of the relief ministry on June 2, 2002. But it was the daily round of the liturgy at noon, which gave a particular spiritual definition to all that went on in the chapel for the other 23 hours of each day. Here are some accounts of what that worship was like, and the role it played, its impact.*

### Sr. Grace—We wanted to be a sanctuary of holiness for the people we served.

At St. Paul's we wanted to be a community. We wanted it to be Christian. Having the Holy Eucharist every day at noon was a huge piece of it. I was in charge of this daily liturgy. We had a different priest every day, so I was the verger, the sacristan, the reader, the acolyte, the chief cook and bottle washer for the liturgy every day at noon. We wanted it to be hopeful. We wanted it to be healing. We wanted it to provide everything those workers needed. And we were sorely criticized at certain points for not allowing the public in, for being open only to the rescue workers. But there was no way to be a sanctuary of holiness for the people we were trying to serve and have the public in at the same time.

### Elizabeth Belasco—God used us to do God's caring.

I participated in a couple of the services at St. Paul's and it was a small group. There would be somebody snoring away in a pew, which he badly needed to do, and, I think, God was blessing him that way. Some of us were participating in the liturgy, some were standing in the back, talking quietly, or maybe getting a bite to eat or a massage, or having their feet taken care of. But that's all liturgy, too, because that's God caring, and he uses us to do that caring. While none of us served for the sake of being appreciated, we were all touched by this service. I realize my life has changed—my spirituality has grown—I hope I never have to undergo another experience like this—but my life has been enriched, and I praise God for this.

Please pray for all who have suffered losses, those who continue to be traumatized by the day, and for the ministries of those of us who continue to serve God's Kingdom. Please also pray, as I try to do, for those who consider themselves our enemies and wish to do us harm. Pray for peace in our time.

# VISITORS TO ST. PAUL'S CHAPEL

*From the beginning St. Paul's became a place of pilgrimage. Thousands of weeping visitors streamed past the iron fence enclosing the chapel, erecting simple shrines in memory of the lost, leaving messages, signing the white banners placed on the fence by the chapel staff. Throughout the nine months these visitors to the chapel came from around the globe, so its ministry made an impact on the Anglican Communion, the nations of the world, and the life of the entire city. These two examples indicate the scope of that impact.*

### Hiroshima and Nagasaki survivors visit St. Paul's Chapel.

*On April 25, 2002, a group of Japanese survivors of Hiroshima and Nagasaki visited Ground Zero and toured the operations at St. Paul's Chapel. Following the tour they made this statement to their hosts, the 9/11 Families for Peaceful Tomorrows, at the chapel:*

What you have done here is a perfect expression of the spirit of Hiroshima and Nagasaki, where so many survivors renounced revenge forever. Instead, they worked ceaselessly against violence and for the world as a whole. We believe that we share with you the firm conviction that we must help the whole human race make a transition from a "civilization of power" to a "civilization of love." Together let us pledge ourselves to work in solidarity with those around the world who seek peace and equality, and let us promise to do everything in our power to create a twenty-first century free of nuclear weapons, free of terrorism, free of war and all forms of violence.

## December 27, 2001—Mayor Rudolf Giuliani bids farewell to the city from St. Paul's Chapel.

The reason I chose this chapel is because this chapel is thrice-hallowed ground. This is a place of really special importance to people who have a feeling and a sense and an emotion and an understanding of patriotism. This is hallowed by the fact that it was consecrated as a house of God in 1766. And in 1789 George Washington came and after he was inaugurated he prayed right here in this church, which makes it very sacred ground to people who feel what America is all about.

But it was consecrated one more time in 2001 on September 11. On September 11 this chapel remained not only not destroyed, not a single window was broken, not a single thing hurt. And I think there's some very, very special significance in that. The place where George Washington prayed when he became President of the United States stood strong, powerful, untouched, undaunted by the attacks of these people who hate what we stand for. Because what we stand for is so much stronger than they are.

# GIFTS FROM AROUND THE WORLD

*Gifts poured into the chapel from every corner of the nation and from every corner of the globe. A poor Church of England parish in the East End of London that had pioneered social ministry in the Anglican Communion in the nineteenth century sent its own icon of St. Paul to St. Paul's in New York as a symbol of solidarity. During Holy Week, a huge gift arrived from the people of Hawaii, bolstering the spirits of the workers and the bereaved families. Diane (Deener) Matthews, the wife of the rector of Trinity Church, related this story.*

### Deener Matthews—It was one of the miracles of the loaves and fishes

What happened was, to me one of the miracles of the loaves and fishes, a man called Martin Cowart from JFK airport and said, "I'm here and I've brought these things in." And Martin had no idea what to expect. They had 5,000 leis, those beautiful purple orchid leis, and 350 pounds of fresh Ahi tuna, and, I think he even brought seven skids of fresh pineapple. So Martin had to get people out there to pick up the food and get it cooked and distributed. The tuna was fed to the workers at St. Paul's on Good Friday. And the leis were distributed at the Easter Eucharist and at the viewing platform where the bereaved families went, and they were taken to the firehouses for the families of the firefighters who were lost.

*Timothy Farley, who organized the donation, builds houses in Hawaii. A self-described "motley surfer, fisherman type" who was "saved by the love of God," Farley called upon his congregation, the New Hope Christian Fellowship Church of Honolulu, to help gather these gifts. Donations in cash and in kind came from throughout Hawaii—leis from many different lei farms, the tuna from local fish companies, and pineapple from Dole. United Airlines provided the airfreight.*

### Timothy Farley—I don't take any credit; God still does miracles through people.

When I came to St. Paul's at Easter, it was like that miracle of the feeding of the five thousand, only instead of feeding them physically we were feeding their spiritual souls. These people were going through a very difficult time. So for us, it was a time of the pouring out of God's unfailing love and watching His Holy Spirit really take and change that despair to a joy and hope. Every time we gave a lei, it was like watching Jesus bestow his peace, his joy, his comfort and love on the person.

# THE VOLUNTEER EXPERIENCE

*There were about 10,000 volunteers at St. Paul's during the nine months. A large number of family members who had lost loved ones on 9/11 came to volunteer. There were Episcopalians from the parishes of the dioceses of New York, but also from New Jersey, Connecticut, California, South Carolina, Pennsylvania, Oregon, Alabama, and Wyoming and many other parts of the U.S. There were people of all races and all creeds and no creed. The largest volunteer group of all was from B'Nai Jeshuran Temple in Manhattan; one member of that group wanted his son bar mitzvahed at St. Paul's. There were volunteers of all sexual orientations. Seventy members of the Trinity Church staff volunteered on a regular basis. And in addition to the musicians, clergy, grief counselors, podiatrists, and chiropractors, there were lawyers, entrepreneurs, soccer moms, farmers, and the grits ladies who would periodically appear from the South to cook grits for Yankees. They came to pour coffee, sweep floors, take out trash, hand out sweaters, serve 500,000 meals, and simply be a human presence.*

## Linda Hanick—In the middle of the night, everybody's loss rose to the surface.

For a lot of the staff at Trinity Church volunteering at St. Paul's was an important part of helping them to deal with what had happened. My shift was 8:00 at night to 8:00 in the morning, so essentially I pulled straight hours around the clock and that was very difficult. So my volunteering was exclusively at night. There is a space of time in the evening between 2:00 A.M. and 4:00 A.M. when the city is pretty much shut down. Nurses will tell you that it's during that time at hospitals that people will die. And it was during those hours that I had the most real conversations either with volunteers or rescue workers, where it was real quiet and people would tell you where they were when the attack happened, and what they thought about. When people went into St. Paul's, they not only thought about the people who died at the World Trade Center. They brought through that door all the people in their lives they had lost. So in the middle of the night everybody's loss rose to the surface and people would start sharing on that level. People would have conversations that they once would not have had in a million years. That is why Saint Paul's was such a healing place.

St. Paul's helped me reclaim and connect to the experiences I had on the day and night of 9/11. On the morning of 9/11 I was standing on the twenty-fourth floor of Trinity's office building. As we were standing there the second plane buzzed by and went in. It was this huge explosion. I had this incredible experience that I knew that thousands of people had died and the expression that came into my head was the body of the communion of saints. I knew I had witnessed this mass death and yet I felt like those people were there. The people I had lost were there and there was this feeling of the communion of saints, that we were all together.

When I got home that night I was covered in their ashes. My shoes, my clothes, my hair was almost stiff from all the ashes and I hesitated when I went to bed. I had this sense that those who had perished were there on me physically. I had this primal feeling, and I did not want it to go away. I took off my clothes (I actually ended up saving them) and I went to bed. When I woke up in the morning, I lay there still thinking of these people who were physically on me. And when I finally got into the shower, I stayed there for an hour, with the water steaming hot and prayed for all those souls.

I had not thought of that as a Eucharistic thing, but now I do. It came back to me when I walked into St. Paul's Chapel. St. Paul's was a very, very thin place, where there was not a huge division between those of us who were alive and those of us who were dead. I think that is why St. Paul's was so healing. When you walked in you brought all of your loss and you had a sense that it was okay. Sort of the Julian of Norwich thing, all is well and all matter of things will be well.

*Deener Matthews spent many hours as a volunteer at St. Paul's. She described it as "the place where you can shut out all the awful stuff that's happening outside."*

## Deener Matthews—He suddenly realized what he'd been through.

I was talking to a man on the front porch of St. Paul's and he burst into tears. I put my hand on his arm and we moved over into a corner. He said, "Do you know that God is at work in this thing, in spite of how horrible it is? Because someone like you comes from a different world than I come from. I never would have had a chance to know someone like you or you wouldn't have had guts enough to touch me, and take time to talk to me." I said, "Thank you," and then he said, "I think I'm falling apart. This is the first time I've really taken time to realize all I've been doing. I've spent every night at St. Paul's since this happened."

That was in December. He suddenly realized what he'd been through. Before that, I guess that maybe he came in and sat and didn't talk to anybody. I said to him as he was going out the door, "How is it going for you?" That's what triggered it. I'll never forget that beautiful man.

*Salina Sprinkle works in the Trinity Grants Program Office and volunteered often at St. Paul's.*

## Salina Sprinkle—St. Paul's changed everything for me.

I was born and raised in New York. And those towers were really like my life. I grew up with them. And since I've been working at Trinity I've been in and out of those buildings like every day. Every day. I can't believe they're gone. And that so many people were killed for no reason at all.

But St. Paul's was different, another side of what happened. It's like you see this tragedy, and then you see the love and the warmth, and people coming together, and for me, that was what I experienced when I came into this chapel. Actually everything changed for me, because you see all the people coming together, the people coming from different states to help out, the firefighters, the construction workers, you know, and they wanted to talk. Like the construction workers and the firefighters, they came in, and they needed some way to release what they were feeling as they were finding the gruesome things in the rubble. Unfortunately I had to hear gruesome details and at one point one of them was telling me yet another awful story and I started crying, and it started him crying, and I'm like, I'm sorry, but you're telling me things that are really sad. I mean, I couldn't help it. And then we turned away from it, and we got to the point of laughing again, so that made me feel good that I was able to bring him back to another point. So I guess even if you help one person get through what they have been through over there, it's helpful for you, and it helps you to heal quickly.

### James Rossi—Our Staten Island group began our trek down Broadway.

I can only describe my memory of the day as the smell of chlorine and burned electrical wiring. Our section served coffee that was donated by Starbucks. Throughout the day I was wheeling coffee down to St. Paul's from Starbucks on a bellhop's cart that obviously came from the devastated Millennium Hotel.

I was touched by the number of people who stopped by to talk to me. I could sense their need to escape. Some conversations were benign; some were not. I remember one exhausted firefighter coming up to me and, without even saying hello, he began to describe how frustrated he was with the whole operation. He took a bottle of water, thanked me and then blindly shuffled on toward the destruction. You could see the pain and anger in their tired eyes. As the sun went down and night settled in, in a darkened corner of the chapel, a very tired and upset firefighter spoke softly to a chaplain, while tears ran down his cheeks. A nun was playing a familiar hymn softly on the church piano, "Shall We Gather at the River?"

At about 8:30, our Staten Island group gathered our belongings and began our trek down Broadway to the ferry. As we passed Cortland Street I spied a bizarre image in the remains of what was once the south tower. Some sort of fabric, perhaps a curtain, was flapping gently in the breeze of a charred window. An odd reminder to me of the humanity that was lost in this tragedy. I saw tears in the eyes of my friends as we continued to walk to the ferry in silence—these symbols of the strength of the city were gone forever. I wondered if life would ever be the same again.

### Bill Tully—There were quite a few St. Bart's volunteers over time.

At least 112 St. Bart's volunteers worked in shifts and took regular times, and a number of people continued to volunteer until St. Paul's was closed. They made their own commitment to go and be a part of it. St. Paul's will forever be in a lot of our people's hearts, and will be thought of in a very profound way. And some of these people became so attached that they felt that they should be members consulted on decisions. We got some wads of cash and sent people to rent trucks and to go to big markets and clean them out of food for St. Paul's. So in this way, during this time, through St. Paul's, St. Bart's way up in midtown, had this interesting side ministry at Ground Zero. This is what happened in churches during this time, and it now seems heroic.

*Some of those who volunteered at St. Paul's did so at great personal cost. Carolyn Montgomery and her partner Lea Ferant were running a catering firm on 9/11. They went to St. Paul's with an early group of volunteers from St. Clement's Church in Manhattan.*

## Carolyn Montgomery—We spent our entire life savings staying afloat.

We met Martin Cowart and he recognized my partner who's kind of a celebrity chef in New York. Chefs know each other, and he happened to know her. He was organizing the food service at St. Paul's, and she said "Look we'd really like to cook." And he said, "Well very few people can cook. They're really being careful; the health department's really coming in." He knew that Lea and I owned a catering company so he called us into service and we started going there from between two to four days a week, sometimes six days a week if they needed us. That lasted through December.

In our catering company, we didn't have any business. We spent our entire life savings staying afloat for those few months. We were a small business. We were not sure what to do; we knew we wanted to do something to help. We were lucky enough to find a way to do it and we really didn't think much about the fact that we had no income for four months.

The whole experience made us both realize that we needed a change. We had been doing nothing but catering to the rich and famous. We decided that we should try to find a job that was meaningful. So we got a job with United Way, teaching homeless people to cook. That was a good segue back into working life. It felt like the right thing to be doing after we experienced what we did down at Ground Zero.

*Some of the work at St. Paul's was hard physical labor—hauling supplies or food in and out of the chapel, filling and refilling coffee urns, hanging posters and banners on any available wall space. The podiatrists and chiropractors and massage therapists often saw more clients in a day there than they saw on a typical day in their regular offices. Volunteers also absorbed the misery of the workers to whom they ministered, often unwittingly taking upon themselves another's emotional burdens. Massage therapist Rebecca Scott described her encounter with one man, then talked of the emotional highs and lows of her work in the chapel.*

## Rebecca Scott—This is one of the most beautiful places in the world to be.

I was giving a massage to one man who had started working shifts out at the landfill. He talked about how lonely and isolating it was because you had to have this incredible protective gear on, so you couldn't have a conversation with anyone. You're in a suit with a mask so even though you're working side by side with someone else you can't talk to them because they can't hear you. The main part of your job was sifting through debris looking for any part of a human body, or anything that had belonged to a human being. He said also there was no way to get away from it during your shift there because any place that you could go to get something to eat was far away. So he'd end up bringing something to eat. The days that he was there he was so immersed in it it was really hard.

St. Paul's felt to me like one of the most beautiful places in the world to be. In a fairly short period of time all this artwork came from children all over the world. And there were letters from children from all over the world and banners from people all over the world. You could feel it when you were there. There's this light that emanates from it that's really exquisite. That's one reason why I would go do a shift and I would stay longer than I had planned to. I would always be so surprised when I got home and woke up totally exhausted the next day because I never felt exhaustion when I was there. There was an energy that held me up.

I would literally walk out the door and start crying. Sometimes I would not get on the subway, I would walk to Canal Street. And I would cry all the way home. I would be home and I was crying. The minute I walked out of that light, everything about the whole day hit me and I cried for hours. I never felt it when I was there. It wasn't ever a strain, no matter how long I stayed.

I really believe that we were held up by the prayers of people.

*Many volunteers came from nearby Connecticut and New Jersey. The rector of Christ Episcopal Church in Guilford, Connecticut, speaks of presence, sanctuary, and the role of a volunteer clergy chaplain.*

## Norman Macleod—The word made flesh engulfs them.

My role at St. Paul's was what is called a "ministry of presence." Some people draw comfort from seeing a priest in the neighborhood of what is still a vast unmarked grave. While much of the work at Ground Zero became routine, the search for bodies and their recovery never became routine. The smell in the air and the dust and ashes were a constant reminder that this was a place in desperate need of the holy. Some people wanted to talk. Others wanted only to eat and sleep in silence.

There was another reaction to this sanctuary, one that moved me most. Some workers stood, completely still, for minutes at a time, simply taking it all in. They gazed at what they saw inside St. Paul's—the classical lines of the architecture, the countless messages of thanks, the enfolding atmosphere of beauty and peace. These people I left alone, because I was convinced they were having a direct experience of the holy, of the Word made flesh. The Word made flesh engulfs them, through beauty, food, loving touch, a place to rest, and not least, signs everywhere of the love of children.

St. Paul's Chapel granted us a vision of how love can transform and begin to heal.


*Tara and Michael Bane lived in Yardley, Pennsylvania, but he worked in the World Trade Center. Her last memory of Michael was when he said goodbye at 5:00 A.M. as he left for work. For days she clung to the hope that he had not made it into the office on time, but finally she realized he would not be coming home. In her grief, she discovered two other women in Yardley who had also lost their husbands in the tragedy. One of those women, Fiona "Mikki" Havlish, persuaded her to come to work a shift at St. Paul's.*

## Tara Bane—I thought, "Oh, this isn't going to help much."

I think it was in January that we came. I still wasn't sleeping completely through the night and was very emotional and drained most of the time. It was a twelve-hour shift, and I remember being very excited about it. When we all came in and I was in awe, you know, I looked around and I was amazed at all the action, all of the good energy, and all of the pictures and the notes and the drawings and the banners that were sent. But yet it was so quiet.

We sat and listened to what we could do and I thought, "Oh, this isn't going to help much." I got a little frustrated at first, because I wanted to help a lot more. I took charge of a table where volunteers were handing out socks and sweatshirts and things that the workers might need. I sat there and watched firemen and the police come in, and I kind of was in awe of them. I didn't know what to say to them. I was not very happy then, and it was hard for me to be happy, and they wanted someone to greet them. It was a difficult because I didn't want to be fake, and yet it was still very emotional for me. But I remember being struck by their faces when they walked in the church. It was scary actually. Their faces were so blank, deadened looking.

But after awhile I'd see a group come in looking like that and they would sit and rest and they would eat something and talk, and when I saw them leave, they'd be smiling. And, you know, when I saw that first group come in and then leave, and I thought, "Okay, well, I might not be making them smile, but I'm a part of this huge network here that is doing something for them." And so then I felt much better about being there.

And it was a little eerie. I was reluctant to talk to any of them. I didn't want to bother them, and yet at that point, I still had so many questions about Ground Zero and the buildings and the day. I think I'll always have those questions. And there will be a time and a place and a person that I'll be able to ask all those questions.

I felt terrible, because the shift was twelve hours, and I couldn't ... I mean, emotionally it was difficult in the midst of what I was dealing with, and yet I wanted to help so badly. And I think we conked out maybe about nine hours into the shift and I said, "I need to leave now." I did come back a few other times.

I'm a New Yorker, originally. And I grew up, not knowing, really, what community was about. Then we lived in a town where my husband and I were very quiet, we didn't have a large group of people there. And after the events of 9/11, I really learned what it was, what it means to have a community, and be a part of a community. And coming here was a reinforcement of that. And I will be forever appreciative of everyone's support, appreciative myself, as someone who lost someone, and for the support that people gave to the rescue workers, and the encouragement that people gave for this church to continue with the work it did. I have a lot of happy memories from being there. Just feeling so special, that I had a chance to do that.

*The Rev. Stephen L. White, Episcopal chaplain at Princeton University, brought some of his students to volunteer at St. Paul's.*

## Steve White—This was Christ's church in all its messiness.

At St. Paul's I attended mass with the most incredible hodgepodge of humanity I've ever seen gathered in a church—-many of whom were oblivious to the mass going on in their midst. There were rescue workers sleeping or eating lunch—-some of them Jews wearing yarmulkes under their fire helmets. There were National Guard troops from the farms and forests of upstate New York looking very young and lost in the big city. Some of the rescue workers who had not shown much interest in the mass when it began found themselves drawn into the ancient prayers that promise life forever with God and ended up taking communion with tears in their eyes. This was Christ's church in all its messiness, diversity, ambiguity, brokenness, and holiness. And it was truly beautiful.

In the days following the disaster the question was often asked "Why do bad things like this happen?" One answer is, of course, that we have the gift of freedom from God and sometimes we choose to do very evil things. But today I saw much evidence of the love of humanity for one another and caring for one another. So we might as well ask "Why do good things like this happen." And the answer is, of course, that God's love for us is more powerful than any evil.

*A lay volunteer from the Church of the Advent, Spartanburg, South Carolina, describes what she learned at St. Paul's from November 25–30, 2001*

## Katherine Jeter—We shared a kaleidoscope of emotions.

During each hour of every day at St. Paul's Chapel we observed and often shared a kaleidoscope of emotions: shock again and again; profound sadness at the stories we heard; steely determination to keep going, we on our tired feet and legs, they on their long and difficult shifts. The incessant noise of the wrecking ball, heavy machinery, fire engine sirens, and dump trucks intruded on our peaceful sanctuary whenever doors were left open. Love abounded. We loved. They loved in return. We loved each other. For most of us this was our first opportunity to be Jesus to strangers of all races, sexual persuasions, religious preferences, and class. It was transforming and transfiguring.

It was only a small balm and a tiny bandage that I was able to apply to my heartbroken city and to the stunned and sorrowful throngs who made their pilgrimage to the site. But it came from *his* heart through mine. It was only a week. It wasn't to the least of these that we gave. We reached out to some of *his* bravest and best. I am embarrassed by their gratitude, but I know that this is how the world is when *his* love prevails.

Five things made this a life-changing experience for me:

- I see sanitation workers, policemen and women, firefighters on every street corner in America with new interest, respect, and appreciation.
- I experienced what it meant to be "the church." Absent was bickering about Rite I or Rite II, traditional or renewal hymns.
- I am persuaded that my gifts are hospitality and encouragement.
- I have seen that evangelism requires few words.
- I lived the truth of this statement: "We are not the same when we have lived in community. We teach each other. We are changed."

## Dennis Fisin—We had these Southern ladies come regularly to cook grits.

We had these Southern ladies come regularly, with only one purpose: to cook the grits. Nothing else. The beauty of it was that we were able to provide them with that particular purpose. They wanted to cook grits for the men of New York City. They literally had to drop whatever they were doing to come in and volunteer. And they would do night shifts, because you can only make grits for the morning, so they had to do the night shift. That is something that always blew my mind. And they did this three times over a six-month period, that's a lot. They came to St. Paul's for one specific purpose: grits. They said, "Look, we're going to be good at making grits." That was the beauty of St. Paul's; it empowered volunteers to do exactly what they thought they were good at. It was a space that allowed people's gifts to come out.

**Carter Booth and Diane Reiners—St. Paul's was a real lesson in letting go.**

The model of volunteering that emerged at St. Paul's was this: people came up with solutions even if you didn't think they were the best solutions. St. Paul's was a real lesson in letting go, and a real comfort to realize the magic that people create. We have all these examples—the grits being one. People could take ownership of what they did. When people walked out the door after volunteering we wanted them to turn around to us and say, "Wow! Look what we did." That was important. And in order to feel that, they had to be able to be creative.

*St. Peter's Episcopal Church in Sheridan, Wyoming, contributed about five percent of its annual budget in 2001 to the work of St. Paul's. Its rector traveled to New York to serve as a volunteer and bring the experience back to his people in this sermon.*

**David Duprey—I simply stood there and I cried.**

St. Paul's Chapel was the church. All down the walls and aisles were first aid supplies and food stored on tables. Beautiful people were working these tables with gentle smiles. Clergy walked through the place visiting with people and offering care. As I stood at the back of the church I tried to take it all in for you. I simply stood there and I cried, as I took in each image; trying to remember it; trying to figure out how I would describe it.

Before I left, I spoke to a dear woman named Katherine, who was the coordinator of the ministry that day. I admired her smile—the way she had earned that smile by her many hours there—and the way she shared that smile. I thanked her. She thanked us for our contribution. It told her that she was like a beautiful flower rising up from all this tragedy.

I saw the church that day. When I walked through the doors of St. Paul's I saw the Gospel of Christ at work, both inside the church and at Ground Zero. I saw the church there and I see the church here, in front of me.

Today when you come forward for the Eucharist, please seal in your soul the images I have shared with you, and commit your heart to praying for these saints. Would you remember that our God—our awesome and powerful God—our meek and tender God—opens doors that no one can close, and closes doors that no one can open?

# RESCUE WORKERS RESPOND TO ST. PAUL'S

### Manny Rodriguez, construction worker—Nothing but kisses and hugs!

St. Paul's has done more than what I can expect. They give me a bed to sleep on at night. And I'm up at five in the morning, I get a wake-up call and have my little breakfast and I'm right out of the church and right back down into the hole. And that's been my routine since October. And the staff here is beautiful. And all those people who walk through the church. Nothing but kisses and hugs. We'd come in tired and beat out and leave new men.

### Daniel Tuthill, fireman—Everyone has put their footprint on St. Paul's.

I thank St. Paul's for actually being what a church should be, not a museum, as most of them are. We have all made this church our own. Everyone has put their footprint on it one way of another, and it will always be close in our hearts, and I want to thank the diocese for having the courage to do this.

*Chosen as one of the New York "heroes" to appear on the Oprah Winfrey show, police officer Gail Douglas called St. Paul's "an oasis of heaven in the midst of hell." In the first few weeks after 9/11 thousands of cards and letters and gifts from all over the world began to arrive at St. Paul's. By Christmas the volume of cards and letters had risen to a thousand a week. A majority of these were from children, and they were displayed on the walls of the chapel, along with flags, banners, and artwork. These letters became a way in which the world touched the workers at Ground Zero directly.*

### Gail Douglas, policewoman—What touches me is the letters from the children.

What touched me at St. Paul's were the letters from the children. I write the children back. I've gotten responses back from Arizona, Tennessee, and Kentucky, places I have never been in my life. These letters come from the heart and they have remade my heart. The cards and letters covered every square inch of the chapel, and they covered every square inch of my heart. They lifted my spirits. They were a sign of hope. For us they said the whole world was with us; and that made all the difference in the world.

## A fireman—This place was a bit of sanity in an insane environment.

This church has meant so much to all the relief workers. I have tried to explain this to my family, what it was like when you come in here at two o'clock in the morning, you're beat down, and you'll have somebody there lightly singing, or a flute going, or a cello. Someone to sit and talk to. This place was a bit of sanity in such an insane environment. And all the letters and the declarations around here that came from throughout the whole country, every part, in the pew, the banners, it's hard to explain it. And I wanted my family to experience this also.

## St. Paul's Chapel and Trinity Parish

*St. Paul's Chapel is a part of Trinity Parish, not an independent religious institution. Throughout its long history, Trinity had added new chapels in other parts of the city as New York grew. In addition, with the coming of industrialization, urbanization, and urban dislocation, Trinity founded additional institutions to meet the social and human needs of the city. Some of these—St. Margaret's House for the elderly, John Heuss House for the chronically mentally ill homeless—played a role in the response to 9/11. But St. Paul's was unique in that though it was Trinity's longest-standing place of worship, within its walls a new social institution was created to respond to the relief effort at Ground Zero. The experiment of this institution lasted nine months; St. Paul's in this short period became a laboratory, teaching lessons to other churches that might be faced with terror and cataclysm. September 2001–June 2002 was also the story of how a major religious institution contained this experiment within its complex system of religious, social, artistic, and civic service.*

**Peter Gudiatis—A neighbor from across the street reflects on the significance of the chapel.**

Seeing a church that I had worked in as a seminarian and understanding the history of survival that had taken place at the World Trade Center I think was fairly miraculous at some level. To take a sacred space, a sanctuary devoted to worship and turn it into a warehouse of crazy things, boxes of socks and boots and tables covered with Chap Stick and anything else that someone might need as a relief worker for months was really a profound experience of what the church is physically, but at the same time also what it's supposed to be spiritually. It really was a place of healing. It really was a place of renewal and worship in a very objective way. What you witnessed across the street was the hope that you saw in the neighborhood. It became a shrine. This sort of shrine, this healing place, this sort of place that transformed what took place at Ground Zero for so many people points forward to a renewal in our church that does not stop here.

*Dall Forsythe, the chief administrative officer of the Diocese of New York, is a former member of the vestry of Trinity Church.*

**Dall Forsythe—Trinity and St. Paul's responded in transformingly positive ways.**

It was very moving to see what happened at Trinity, because first, this huge, strong, wonderful church was—although not physically damaged—knocked off its feet in terribly important ways. But then as it responded, sometimes in a few days, like at St. Paul's, other times, over a longer period, as the whole enterprise mobilized, it was very moving to see how this happened. Because I think at first Trinity and St. Paul's were also victims of the terrorist attack. But then the victims responded, not only in a positive way, but in a way that was almost unexpectedly and transformingly positive, and in other ways, as at St. Paul's, in ways that were very, very moving.

*The vicar of Trinity Church, the Rev. Samuel Johnson Howard, was directly responsible for St. Paul's in the parish's administrative structure. He speaks about how the experiment existed within the larger enterprise.*

## John Howard—I felt myself reacting a lot during those nine months.

As vicar of Trinity Church and vicar of St. Paul's Chapel I felt myself reacting a lot during those nine months. I was trying to make sure that fire codes were observed and that registers were kept of who was there, and that the medical personnel all had licenses on file—doing all those mundane things. That inevitably felt like putting on the brakes to people for whom the ministry of St. Paul's was the largest opportunity for ministry in their lives, as it was for all of us. As a manager I needed them to know about those brakes, but that is where there was a lot of tension, between experiment and brakes. So we had experiment bumping up against an institution that feels itself very self-consciously to be a steward of a place and a tradition that has served this city for three hundred years.

In retrospect, we have got to look at what those nine months did to us in terms of our relationship with God, our anxiety, and how we experience the goodness and the grace of God. The answer is that out of all the tension and chaos we experienced at times, there was born a ministry of reconciliation. Reconciliation, that is the word—that is the ministry that was held up at St. Paul's during those nine months. The people from around the nations of the world are still being called to St. Paul's to learn what it means to be reconciling. To learn what it means to be ambassadors for Christ. To learn what it means to tap that gracefulness, that goodness of God for our own lives and for our own time of uncertainty, anxiety, and vulnerability.

*Ultimately, the rector of Trinity Church, the Rev. Dr. Daniel P. Matthews, holds responsibility for all the various institutions that make up Trinity Parish. He must mediate conflicting claims for time and for resources and his is the public voice that speaks for Trinity to the wider world.*

**Dan Matthews—In some deep sense, this church has always seen itself as a giving center.**

When we started out, at that time, we thought we were serving a very crucial and important need for the firefighters and the rescue workers and the police, for a brief time. What was the brief time? We didn't know. Was it going to last a week or two or three or four or six weeks? We never could have imagined it would go on and that it got deeper and richer. On the other hand, there were those conflicting moments of—can this actually be happening to St. Paul's? So to say, "When are you going to close it?" was a continuous sort of thing. How long is this going to go on?

It was an emergency to which we were responding with aid. We were in chaos. Our scholar in residence here, Dr. Burnham, said that's the basis of chaos theory: that chaos reigns until it has its own self-organizing systems. The self-organizing system took over at St. Paul's and began to make sense of the chaos. But we knew at the time it was spirit-filled. It was dedication. At one moment it was chaos, and the chaos turned into a self-organizing creative spiritual center.

At St. Paul's love—in the form of boots, coffee, a massage—was given freely, with no strings attached, by all sorts of people—doctors, lawyers, merchants. The place was full of love. It was a highly paid lawyer helping a street person. And that was magic. It was a spiritual high. It was a taste of the Kingdom of God. It was a glimpse of the way heaven will be.

And this, though it did not last beyond nine months, was in some way consistent with the 300-year history of Trinity Church, which was founded by the free gift of an English monarch to a village in America. There's some deep sense in which this church has always seen itself as a giving center. This church, over the course of 300 years, has given away approximately ninety-six per cent of its endowment in the service of others; that is unusual. I think that kind of sense of always being responsible to give, was deeply embedded in the psyche of this place, and it came to the surface again in 2001. There wasn't any thinking through this. There wasn't any "we're changing the axioms." The axioms were already there.

*Professor Kenneth Jackson of Columbia University, as both a vestry member of Trinity Church and President of the New-York Historical Society, is in a unique position to place the activities at St. Paul's within an historical perspective.*

## Kenneth Jackson—These religious structures played a major role.

September 11 scared a lot of people. Suddenly the city, once again, is seen as something that is dangerous. It makes us now think of skyscrapers as dangerous.

But I think there have been a few positive things to come out of it. Certainly the human response, the religious response from Trinity and St. Paul's. The urgency of so many volunteers to come to St. Paul's.

It is both ironic and appropriate that on 9/11, these two buildings, Trinity and St. Paul's, these two religious structures in the symbolic business heart of capitalism of the world, played a major role. Over the years all the other major churches of Lower Manhattan had moved uptown as the population shifted. But Trinity and St. Paul's stayed there. And of course Trinity has a particular patrimony and mandate and its own history, so it stayed. But here it is on September 11, 2001 and because of all of history in some ways, and because of an accident, they are there. And in this world disaster in which billions of people are focusing on Lower Manhattan—there are Trinity and St. Paul's. And then of course Trinity is so important while the event happens. It becomes a place of refuge for people who think the world is about to end. For all they know, there is a nuclear attack going on. They go into Trinity to pray, to spend their last moments.

But I think it was really the historic moment of this great religious institution that it was there and it was able to respond. I don't think it was in the stars that St. Paul's Chapel should be the center for recovery right after that. But it was. It was at the right place. It seemed appropriate. It wasn't an office building. It was a church. It was a place of God and people could see that. And yet it was doing what a place of God ought to do, which is to respond to human beings in their moment of need. And so I think Trinity and St. Paul's did what they should have done. But they did it and I think they deserve honor and glory for stepping up and not asking, "Who's paying for these lights anyway? What happens when somebody slips on one of these candy bars and breaks his neck? Is somebody going to sue us for this? What's happening to our precious relics? The place is being unintentionally trashed."

The church did not ask itself those kinds of questions, the church said instead, "What we can do now is provide the space, and so let's do it. We can fix it up later." And that's exactly what the church did.

Ultimately I hope that people will take a more positive view of religion from all of this. I know many people who are usually not religious say "How can there be a God who allows this to happen? I know that there was a perfectly wonderful twenty-three-year- old man or woman, up there on the ninety-ninth floor who had everything to live for and how could a merciful God allow this to happen?" What I hope is that people will believe that it is not God who piloted those airliners. And God does not save everyone. But what we need to do is have the strength to deal with whatever emergency or whatever tragedy comes our way. We can't be free of that. I think all we can do is try to face the future confidently. And I think in some ways the church is a model. We could have closed St. Paul's a long time before the World Trade Center happened. In some ways Trinity was paying a debt. Keeping this little church open was a gift to the people of the United States and the people of New York City.

# 4
# OTHER MINISTRIES

## THE MORGUE

*Within the Episcopal Diocese of New York, many other active ministries emerged in response to the attack. Some were long-term, specialized ministries, others were new directions taken by individuals or churches. But in one way or another, each of these ministries called forth new understandings of discipleship, of commitment, of the call to serve.*

*The ministry at the Morgue was one of the most demanding commitments. In the early hours after the collapse of the Twin Towers, authorities set up a temporary Morgue near the site to receive and label bodies before they were transported to the City Morgue near Bellevue Hospital. The site of that Morgue changed during the early weeks, until it was finally set in a trailer on the southeast edge of Ground Zero. All bodies and body parts were brought to that Morgue, labeled as to where they had been found, and checked by the Port Authority and the crime scene investigators and an officer from the Fire, Police, or EMS department if the person had been a member of one of those services. Then the bodies were sent to the City Medical Examiner's site near Bellevue Hospital for identification.*

*Chaplains were stationed at the Morgue twenty-four hours a day. The chaplain went into the site when a body was discovered, blessed it there, then accompanied the procession that brought the body out and said prayers over the body when it was brought into the Morgue and again when it was loaded into the ambulance to be taken to the City Morgue. The interim time was spent in the trailer, talking to the workers there.*

*At the beginning of November, the Reverend Tom Faulkner, priest associate at St. James' Church, Manhattan became the Red Cross Officer in Charge of the Morgue Chaplaincy. Faulkner literally stumbled into that job. He had come into the Morgue trailer to find the Red Cross Chaplain.*

## Tom Faulkner—Stumbled into a job

I opened the door and a fellow there said, "What do you want?" Well I knew I was in a different environment, one that was foreign to me. I centered myself as quickly as I could. He was the Red Cross chaplain responsible for the chaplains at the morgue. He had been at the Pentagon for ten days, flew up to New York and now was at the end of his two-week shift at Ground Zero. He was exhausted but determined to know who I was and why was I there. As he was checking me out, he got a call from the Fire Department that they found the remains of a fireman and he had to go to the pit. He said to me, "You wait here," I waited there in this morgue which smelled very sweetly from the perfumed candles that were lit. He came back within half an hour with a body bag in which were the remains of a fireman, a body bag draped with an American flag. He said, "You stand here with me." I got the message that whatever was going to happen next, he wanted me with him. That was the first blessing of remains that I participated in. The body bag was opened and there were the remains of a fireman, a full body. I, of course, had never seen anything like this before. My heart was beating out of my chest.

After all the identification and registration was done, then the body bag was zipped up again and the American flag was placed back on it. It then was escorted to an ambulance that took it to the morgue at Bellevue Hospital. At the end of this, about 5:30 P.M., this chaplain said to me, "Can you take over for me tonight? I've been doing twenty-four-hour shifts and I'm exhausted. I have to have some relief." He and I, at that moment, connected.

*Faulkner took over that night, and eventually was asked by the Red Cross to become the permanent head, a job he held until the recovery site was closed in June, 2002.*

*Faulkner's team consisted of about sixty chaplains from many faiths, though Episcopal priests and deacons were by far the majority. Most people signed up to do the same eight-hour shift every week or every other week. The work was grueling.*

WILL THE DUST PRAISE YOU?

*Betty Belasco, a seventy-one-year-old retired teacher and permanent deacon took regular shifts at the Morgue for months.*

## Betty Belasco—The first thing that struck me was the odors.

The first thing that struck me was the odors. These were not really odors of decomposition because there wasn't that much decomposition. The temperature was so high that it killed off most of the bacteria. So, there wasn't that. I can't really describe the odor. It was not a good one. Several of us used a little Vicks VapoRub here or wore the little masks with it. And we burned candles in the Morgue to dispel the odors.

## Tom Synan—One tough moment, one humorous moment.

The toughest moment for me was the time when we found a full body. And I will never forget it. The medical examiner put his hand in the pocket and pulled out the guy's ID. And, to see the picture of this fresh faced, young kid, probably about twenty-five years old, that here are his remains now. It brought it home. It was the full magnitude of life. What a loss. And what a crime. That was seeing real death.

One humorous moment came when I was being driven down into the Pit, by this fireman who was sort of crazy, but in that line of work, that's kind of what some of them are. And, he's driving the Gator down like a maniac, and, we went as far as the group path, then off the path, and as far as he could take the thing. Then he pulls the brake, we go sliding. I thought the thing was going to roll over. Then we come to a stop. He leans over to me and says, "I scared ye, Father, didn't I?" And another fireman in the back says to him, "What are you talkin' about? Priests don't get scared." And I said, "Well, maybe we're a little bit like firemen. If we are scared, we're going to try to not let you see it." Then the crazy driver interrupted, "You'd be afraid, though, if you met the devil." And I said, "Well, I'm not quite sure how I'd feel if I met the devil." And of course this is a whole lead-up, because he had something he wanted to say, so he said, "I'll tell you, Father, if I met the devil, I wouldn't be afraid. You want to know why?" I said, "Sure." And he said, "That's proof there's a God."

*Volunteers rarely mentioned it but there was certainly an economic cost to this ministry. For the Rev. Denise Mantell, rector of Trinity Church, Matawan, New Jersey, working with the Fire Department was in her blood—her brothers, sister, and father were all firefighters. She herself had served as chaplain to two different fire companies. Her first day as a volunteer at Ground Zero was September 14 and she continued to serve, at the Morgue and at St. Paul's, for at least one day a week until the cessation of work the following June. That meant a ninety-minute commute by train each way from Southern New Jersey on top of the eight-hour shift at the Morgue—often combined with another twelve-hour shift at St. Paul's.*

## Denise Mantell—It cost me a considerable amount of money.

As a matter of fact, it cost me a considerable amount of money. I know that because I'm doing my taxes! Every time I went in there it would cost $20 to $30. And if you figure, the first couple of months, it was as much as twice a week, and from then on at least once a week. And then there was the stuff that you picked up that was needed at the site. Sometimes people gave you a break on that, sometimes not.

And then, sometimes after a particularly horrific day, it's ten o'clock at night and Houlihan's Bar is open in Penn Station and you want to go in and have a glass of beer or a glass of wine. Not that we did that regularly or anything but, you know, you've missed the train, you've got an hour—let's go in and have a glass of wine. Yeah, it was pretty expensive. A couple of thousand dollars at least.

There was so much. There was going down into the Pit, freezing, watching people doing the same thing. There was the frustration of thinking, "Why did we find them now, when we can't do anything?" And there was the supporting ministry that went with that—when you go out and you have to talk to somebody because the skeleton that has been unearthed on the floor is obviously that of a child. It was not easy. It was not easy with what you saw, with what you smelled, with going down into the Pit.

Okay—the frustration. When they opened up the federal building, which was one of the last ones that they opened up because of the structural lack of integrity. You walked in and there were a bunch of human remains. And then you walked across the room and opened the doors into the garage and there were untouched automobiles. Perfectly preserved—you could drive them off!

Why was it important to do this work? When you've got a society who sees you as marginally unimportant, and that's a great number of the population, at least here on the East Coast, all of a sudden to become an integral part of the team again—not only at the Pit but within your parish, within the hospital, the nursing home. What was it Bob Dylan said? "Religion's for the dying." When you're faced with your mortality, all of a sudden, it becomes important again. And to be able to assist people in being able to deal with that is important to us.

## Tom Faulkner—In retrospect.

We became a community of clergy who knew what we were doing. We all knew that when we were at an examination table with remains, some of which could be very disturbing and very rank in terms of smell, we were dealing with the wild emotions of ourselves and the other people gathered with us. We were dealing with a horrific disaster site. We were dealing with the glory of people working together and being together as God's children. We were empowered by God's spirit; we felt that we absolutely knew that this was sacred space.

We all have our defenses, our ways of protecting ourselves. We put up these defenses and that really keeps us in a safe secure self-controlled environment. What a disaster does, is it throws you up against a terrible reality and the defenses start to break down. All of a sudden there is a little opening. Prejudices break down, priorities change because you're up against this disaster. At that moment, there's the possibility for God to enter in, in remarkable ways, and there's a way for other people to enter in and fear to enter into the large love of people. There are remarkable moments of transformation.

*After leaving Ground Zero, the human remains were taken to a field operation center set up next to the Medical Examiner's building at Bellevue Hospital for identification. Almost from the beginning, family members sought information there and the Rev. Betsee Parker, an Episcopal priest, began a ministry of presence there. She was joined by the Rev. Charles Flood who came each week from Philadelphia to hold an interfaith memorial service. Together they set up a chaplaincy program connected to the Office of the Chief Medical Examiner and recruited Christian, Jewish, Muslim and Buddhist volunteers to minister to the family members and the medical and forensic scientists who continued the task of identification. A chapel has been constructed at the entrance to the site and volunteers were available there for counseling. Mary Ellen Blizzard, a laywoman from St. Luke in the Fields, is one such volunteer.*

### Mary Ellen Blizzard—It strengthens your own faith.

When you do interfaith work, it strengthens your own faith. It's made me more drawn to the sacraments, to the restitution that we feel in receiving the body and blood of Christ. It's made me aware that there's very little you can say. People need someone to be there with them but very little more than that. I've become aware of how we can step in each other's circles, how, when you've had a life-changing experience even if it is unspoken, you can easily be welcomed into someone's circle to share and to hear about their journey. And it's made me see the real tenderness of how people have been there for one another. Recently, in the Morgue chapel, a family came in with flowers. Another woman was there alone and she didn't have flowers to put down on the altar. The family shared theirs with her. Whenever the families encountered each other, they didn't need us at all. They started talking and sharing. That's the deepest bond—they have a like experience

# MINISTRY TO MARINERS—
# SEAMEN'S CHURCH INSTITUTE

*Even while the Seamen's Church Institute was organizing food delivery in lower Manhattan, some staff members assisted by many volunteers had another task in Port Newark—to minister to the seafarers who were detained on their ships immediately after 9/11. The restrictions on port leave were not eased until after Christmas. Mariners rely on their time in port to get needed supplies and to telephone family members. They enjoy visiting the city and relaxing on dry land. Confined to the ships, often having little*

*access to news in their native languages, many of them feared official or non-official
retaliation for a deed for which they were not responsible.*

*SCI staff convinced the authorities to allow them to board the vessels to see what they
could do for the detainees. They brought cell phones to allow the workers to call families
in many lands; they brought treats and toilet items and newspapers in several
languages. Chaplains led worship services on some of the ships and were available to
talk to the anxious and fearful seafarers. The Rev. Jean Smith had charge of the Port
Newark operations of SCI.*

## Jean Smith—These are our brothers and our sisters.

These people are Filipino and Pakistani and Honduran. These are our brothers and our
sisters who in some ways have been victimized. We could even say that they are being
treated as terrorists. In their minds they are being treated as terrorists.

*Bob Miller is a New Jersey layman who had worked for the Port Authority for several
years but retired before 9/11. He found a new ministry visiting the merchant seamen
who were confined to their ships.*

## Bob Miller—He's a Muslim and that means we have the same God.

Many times, these merchant seamen are very poor, sometimes only making $500 or
$600 a month. They had dirty clothes, and we'd take them clothes. And we brought cell
phones so they could make calls. When a merchant seaman calls home, first of all he runs
over to the porthole so he can have good access to the cellular signals, and after about a
minute of waiting for the call to be completed, all of a sudden you hear him say, "Hello,
Ma." And that's a universal term, through all the various nationalities and languages.

On one ship in particular I remember, we were all sitting down together and a Filipino
said jokingly to me, "Hey, you don't want to talk to that guy, he's a Muslim." And I said,
"He's a Muslim and that means we have the same God." And that Muslim who was
sitting across the table, he reached across and grabbed my hand. We shook on that and
smiled. They were joking when they said that. They all got along so very well. Different
religions, different nationalities, sitting at the same table, and absolutely no problem.

It was so good to see this. It's so good to be able to shake hands and get to know these people and they get to know that we are human beings, we are the children of God.

*Allied to this ministry is the commitment to care for immigrants being held in the U.S. detention center in Elizabeth, New Jersey, just south of Port Newark. The Rt. Rev. Jack Croneberger, Bishop of Newark, has become increasingly concerned about the number of people who are kept there for long periods of time, not allowed to return to their homes nor given legal counsel that could explain to them the reasons for their detention.*

## Jack Croneberger—New meaning to "Give me your tired, your poor..."

I spent a day at the detention center recently and discovered that people who probably should have been processed in seventy-two hours have been there three and a half years. I think we've given a new meaning to "Give me your tired, your poor." Many of them are Colombian; many of them are Asian. They simply come from other countries and the only crime they seem to have committed is that they don't have proper papers and documentation. Trying to get that processed and worked out is taking an unbelievable amount of time. There seems to be no rush to bring some resolution to people who are being detained in there.

What I discovered in the Elizabeth situation is that the Jesuits had gone in and done pastoral work and some Bible study with the people who were there, but they got so passionately involved in people's individual stories that they ultimately got thrown out because they were causing unrest. So what really happened is that Joe Parrish, rector of St. John's Church in Elizabeth, and some of his people did that work in a much quieter way. Some people thought that he sold out, but I think we need people to be outside and lighting candles and sort of shouting and protesting and dealing with Congress to try to get things changed, but we also need the Joe Parrishes who are going to go in quietly and be present there and do that work pastorally. So it's really both/and rather than either/or.

*Clergy and laity from many faiths in Manhattan and Long Island have joined in a similar protest at the Brooklyn Detention Center. As the Rev. Frederick Williams, rector of the Church of the Intercession, explained:*

**Fred Williams—We've become distrustful of our own fundamental freedoms.**

Since 9/11, Justice and Immigration have been randomly picking up people, primarily of Middle Eastern descent. They've incarcerated over 1,200 people and they've been held without access to legal counsel or to their families, and often held incommunicado, that is, without anybody knowing where they were. They haven't been charged with any specific crime. In some instances, a number of people have been deported and their families only notified after the fact.

In the course of this, since 9/11, no one, *not one person* who has been arrested under those circumstances, has been tied to the events of 9/11. So a coalition of concern, across denominational and faith lines, has been demonstrating on a regular basis out at the detention center in Brooklyn. I've been out there because I see this action as a basic denial of our civil rights. In the aftermath of 9/11, the fear and the anger that has been stirred up, has eroded people's confidence in our basic America freedoms. We ought not to be this fearful in a country that's "land of the free and home of the brave." We've become paranoid and distrustful of our own fundamental freedoms.

# FIREFIGHTERS' STAGING AREA—
# HOME PORT, STATEN ISLAND

*Another little-known ministry was one established by the Rev. Fred Fausak, a retired fireman from Staten Island who became an Episcopal deacon. Having served as a firefighter for twenty-eight years, Fred was in a unique position to serve as a liaison between the firemen and the religious community. During the first two months of the rescue operation, the city set up several stations where firefighters doing duty in the Pit assembled each day to be transported to Ground Zero. One such station was established in the Home Port, a former Navy base on Staten Island, for firemen from South Brooklyn and Staten Island and for some of the sanitation workers at the Fresh Kills Landfill where much of the debris was being deposited. The station had showers and beds so many of the men who were working sixteen-hour shifts would simply stay at Home Port during the night and return to work the next day. Local merchants donated food and socks and underwear. Retired firefighters and volunteers came from local churches to serve the food and organize the incoming donations.*

*Fred Fausak is the chaplain of the New York Fire Department Retirees. He and another chaplain set up counseling rooms at the Home Port and scheduled clergy from local churches to be available to the firemen as they returned from Ground Zero.*

## Fred Fausak—There wasn't much being said the first few days.

I spent about eight to twelve hours a day there, I'd get there when one group was coming back, I'd get ready to go with another group. Sometimes I would ride into Ground Zero with the guys and talk. There wasn't much being said the first few days. Everybody was in shock. A lot of people were within themselves. Staten Island lost the highest percentage of firemen, of the 343 firemen that died, 78 of them were Staten Islanders. It was almost double any other borough, except for Nassau County. My company, Rescue 5, lost eleven out of twenty-five men.

I did some counseling and I rode back and forth sometimes with the bus. I'd talk with the men, we'd pray together. It was hard to do the "God talk" at first. There was anger; there was disbelief. You'd ride back and forth on the bus in silence, which is odd for firefighters—they make a joke out of everything. No matter how serious the fire and how hard you worked and how many guys got injured, there was always the joking, I think that was part of the masking. There was so much anger nobody wanted to say anything at first. I felt it wasn't the place to try to force anything.

As time went on, more and more fellows would want to come and pray. Even though they knew I wasn't Catholic, which most of the guys are, we would hold hands, we would pray. To see the firefighters bow down, hold hands and pray—it's not that they're showing signs of weakness, but that sometimes they're afraid—they don't want to let that go. That's when I knew that they needed God, that they needed help.

One of the most amazing things had to be the day they found the cross, the piece of iron that looked like a cross. I had ridden in that day and it was turning night. With the bright lights, it was like every light was on that cross, it was like the Star of David coming down. When we got back that night, we had four rooms at Home Port for counseling, every room had a line. It was amazing how that uplifted us. It showed people that God did care. They were blaming God. Everybody was saying, "Why is God doing this?" The hardest thing was explaining God didn't do this. God does not make these things happen. Man does these things. One of the gifts that God gave us was our free will, some of us choose to be good and some of us choose to be bad. This was the point I kept trying to make. It wasn't God; it was what God gave to us, the free will that we have, gift of being able to make decisions. When I would get this message across, I think a lot of them understood.

# EPISCOPAL CHARITIES

*The urge to do something to respond to this tragedy reached far beyond the borders of New York City. Many people recognized the need for funds, and money began to flow into Episcopal relief agencies. Within the Diocese of New York, Episcopal Charities was designated as the agency to receive and disburse emergency funds and established its 9/11 Fund. As Executive Director, David Shover, explained:*

### David Shover—An outpouring of generosity from around the world.

What was probably most moving to me was that there were people out there who obviously needed to follow an impulse to do something. In most cases these were Episcopalians who wanted to connect to something that was local and something they thought would be in the position to do something useful. We got donations from within the diocese, from churches, congregations and individuals from all over the country, and even from people overseas. We got one response from a Lutheran pastor in a small town on the Baltic Sea in Germany saying that the kids in his church wanted to do something. I think he actually contacted somebody he knew at the cathedral and that person put him in contact with us and we got a contribution and some things the kids had made. There

were lots of stories of people who tracked us down because they wanted to find somebody local and they wanted their money to be put to work immediately.

*Episcopal Charities is a small organization, with a staff of three people, founded six
years ago to enhance outreach efforts of Episcopal congregations by providing financial and technical support for a large number of diocesan organizations and programs.
As donations poured in, the agency had to hire additional caseworkers and become
directly involved in assessing community needs. At the same time, Episcopal Relief and
Development, the church's national assistance agency, decided also to make direct
grants to the dioceses involved in the tragedy. Eventually, Episcopal Charities received
over $440,000 from various independent sources, particularly from Episcopal congre-
gations and $1,400,000 from Episcopal Relief and Development to be used for emer-
gency assistance. Governed by a volunteer board of directors, the agency was able to
act quickly to dispense funds where needed.*

## David Shover—The Holy Spirit was working.

Almost all of our donors said, "We want this money to go to people who otherwise
won't be helped." I think they were hearing about large funds being established for firefighters and police and for the families of people who died in the World Trade Center.
Then we might say the Holy Spirit was working, for we began learning about groups of
people that were exactly those kinds of people. They started to come to us. We made a
decision very early on that we wanted to dispense the money as quickly as possible,
because our donors were giving this for emergency needs. Surprisingly, among all the
faith-based organizations, we seemed to be the only one that moved quickly in that
regard. We went to some organizing meetings early on and many of the church groups
were sitting on big pots of money wondering what to do with it, they were amazed that
we were actually giving it away. I'd like to say we planned all that, but we didn't. It
came to us and we had to respond and we did. In the end, we granted basic assistance
funds to more than 300 families.

*Many grants were made to families of low-income workers who had either perished or
had lost their jobs because of the collapse of the World Trade Center but for some reason*

*did not qualify for or were unwilling to seek recompense from the federal disaster relief fund. There were two interesting groups that were helped in the early months. One was a group of Central and South American workers at the World Trade Center. Many were undocumented aliens, often with families who did not speak English. One large group of such families in Mt. Kisco was being provided with counseling services by a local non-profit organization, Face to Face. Thirty of their undocumented workers were killed, leaving families who had almost no resources, but were unwilling to apply for federal aid, which might jeopardize their immigration status. Confronted with that need, Episcopal Charities established a guideline that continued to be its benchmark policy: recipients would be provided with enough money to allow the family to remain where they were living for three months. Carla Rediker, Executive Director of Face to Face, described one of the families assisted by Episcopal Charities.*

## Carla Redeker—We will never have words enough to express our gratitude.

Two parents were killed, leaving behind a little boy, age three, and an older sister, age twenty. They are now living with and want to stay with their aunt (mom's sister) with whom they are very close and who is a single mom with a young child. The oldest child is very depressed, having nightmares. She was working two jobs full-time in order to get enough money to go to college to study to become a nurse/social worker, but has started working only part-time, both to spend more time with her family and because she is not up to doing more. The little boy is still confused, but doing fairly well.

*Peter Gudaitis, Assistant Director of Episcopal Charities, described another group that received immediate assistance, Egyptian limousine drivers who worked for a company in New Jersey whose principal business was in lower Manhattan.*

## Peter Gudaitis—Assisting a Muslim group.

When the World Trade Center came down, the company lost its business and the drivers were all laid off. Iman Elmahroukey and her husband Moataz were the first to come in for assistance and she became the central person to try to get access to services for the coworkers.

They were humbled by the experience of having to look for help. It was clearly something that they had never had to do before. They were unprepared for it. They didn't really know where to get assistance. They had been very poorly treated at some other assistance venues. Limousine and taxi cab drivers for some reason got sidelined very early on as people who were not going to get a lot of assistance. I'm not really sure what the reasons were for that, but they got turned down quite a bit. We were the first place where they heard, "Yes, we'll help you."

Later on we found out it was really a very humbling experience for them because they had some negative ideas about the Christian church in the United States. Their perception was that Christians here were conservative, nationalistic faith communities that cared for their own people first. I think they were rather shocked that they were now going to get assistance from one of those institutions. But rather quickly Iman realized that our desire to help them was genuine and heartfelt and that we really were concerned about the well-being of this Muslim community in New Jersey. Many people came forth from that community and we helped those who demonstrated a significant financial need.

Some of the Egyptians began to tell us stories about family members who had been detained by the FBI. All of them ended up being released, but in the interim, Iman and Moataz took the detainees' families in and fed them. They were always apologizing for what had been done in the name of the Muslim faith and using examples of how their community had been brought together by the prejudice they'd experienced from other Americans and also by the generosity they had experienced from American Christian groups like Episcopal Charities.

*Dealing with this emergency has wrought definite changes in the work of Episcopal Charities. The agency became more directly involved in casework.*

## David Shover—What the families need is long-term basic financial support.

We developed a program of case management services to discover what resources are available and to try to follow up each family who had received financial assistance, to find out how they're doing, if they need any additional services. We tried to connect them with job placement or job-training organizations. If they were having trouble with their utilities, we would try to put them in touch with people who could help them negotiate with the utility companies. We have found that for many of the families that we helped, their basic need continues to be financial. What they really needed was additional financial basic support because they weren't able to get jobs. As we all know, many of the basic services parts of the economy have not come back and many of these people are not going to be employed for a long time.

*For the future, Episcopal Charities has begun to work cooperatively with Episcopal Social Services and the cathedral's Community Cares program by funding social workers who would work out of those offices to provide case management services, leaving Episcopal Charities with its primary task of raising funds to support such programs. As to what the effort meant to the Charities employees themselves, Peter Gudiatis, who interviewed so many of the applicants for assistance, explained,*

## Peter Gudiatis—The human faces make it real.

I have sat down across the table from a Muslim seeking assistance, a Louisiana woman who worked for years as a maid in the Marriott Hotel, a person of no faith or someone who is Jewish. When I try to put a human face on this tragedy, these are the faces I see. Muslim, Jew, atheist, Christian, American, Mexican, Egyptian, Columbian— those are the human faces this act impacted. It did not harm the U.S. government. It did not harm the United States as a collective. It harmed these individuals. They are the victims. Those human faces are the only things that make it real, the only experience of it that I can take into myself to try to understand how we're going to move forward and heal from this.

Our hope for this country is to honor it as a melting pot, so our hope for the world must be the same, that we can somehow take the strengths of other people's faith traditions, take the strengths of other people's cultures and appreciate them, honor them, hold them up as unique, not try to eradicate them. Here in this country we have a lot of social struggles. We struggle for equity and justice and we often fall far short. But in general we don't come to bear arms against one another. We try to discuss those differences and figure out how we can best interact with one another to honor others yet maintain the integrity of our own beliefs. If we can't be part of that discussion on a global level, if we can't figure out the opportunities to dialogue with these various countries or these various people whom we have somehow insulted or harmed, then this is going to happen again. I think we misunderstand and we are misunderstood, and I hope very profoundly, very deeply, that we can learn about moving forward as global citizens.

*Not all the financial assistance that was administered after 9/11 came through Episcopal Charities. Many individual parishes also made specific gifts to individuals in need.*

### William Tully—One man owned five hot dog carts.

One man owned five hot dog carts that ringed the World Trade Center. He had finally realized his dream. He had a going business. He had a person to work each of these carts, and he said, "Believe it or not, this was quite a good business." And all the carts were destroyed. He was out of business. He was still paying the loans to buy these carts. And he was told that he would eventually get some Small Business Administration and FEMA money. But in the meantime, he was a man living in a Brooklyn neighborhood where three longtime friends of his, firefighters, were dead. He said, "I'm not dead. I'm thankful, but I'm bereft." When he came to us, he said, "I pulled my daughter out of college. I sold a car to pay off the car loan. I'm doing everything I can to try to save my house and my family. I don't know where to turn."

We gave him two cash grants, counseled with him over a period of months and sent a volunteer with him to his Small Business Administration interview to help him fill out the forms. It's not a particularly happy story. The family went through hell for about a year. He's made adjustments. But he is a man who doesn't have an extended family, doesn't have other sources to turn to. One of the people at the Federal Center had told him, "Go to midtown and find one of those big churches, the bigger the better. And walk in and ask them if they can help you." That's how he got here. We gave him the money and said, "When you get your settlement, if you can pay this back, that means we can help somebody else. But this is not a loan. This is a gift. Do with it as you can."

*Episcopalians from across the country opened their pocketbooks with extraordinary generosity to fund this response. An accounting of the gifts contributed to the five major recipients—the Diocese of New York, Episcopal Charities (New York), Episcopal Relief and Development, Seamen's Church Institute, and Trinity Church—indicates that more than $3,500,000 was contributed specifically for 9/11 relief in the metropolitan New York area. An additional amount of over $3,000,000 was contributed to Episcopal Relief and Development for 9/11 with no specific geographic site listed, and much of that was also used for work in New York. Though there were some notable gifts from foundations, corporations and other religious denominations, the vast majority of these contributions came from individuals and parishes across the United States and accounted for more than half of the total amount contributed. Many other New York City parishes also received contributions and disbursed those funds directly to individuals or helping agencies.*

*The monetary grants were supplemented by donations in kind, particularly to the work at St. Paul's Chapel. Steady, long-term gifts came from Eli's Bread, Dallas Brothers BBQ, the Waldorf-Astoria Hotel, Pepsi, Red Bull, Hershey, Starbucks Coffee, Dunkin' Donuts and the Hain Celestial Group (teas), but many other New York City restaurants also donated large numbers of meals and kitchen supplies. Significant donations in kind that came to Seamen's Church Institute included food from the Union Square Cafe, Bloomberg Financial and their caterer, Great Performances, and Stew Leonard's.*

# SPECIAL RELIGIOUS SERVICES

*The magnitude of the loss of life on 9/11 evoked a deep need for communal remembrance. Several corporations lost many employees and their surviving coworkers needed corporate as well as individual ways to express their grief. The power of liturgy to encompass a community's grief and offer consolation has rarely been as deeply felt as it was in the days after 9/11.*

## ST. BARTHOLOMEW'S CHURCH

*Though the firm of JP Morgan Chase had lost only one employee in the disaster, the fact that as a Wall Street banking firm they had done business with so many of the people who perished prompted the management to hold a service of remembrance for their down-town employees. One of the managers called Bill Tully, rector of St. Bartholomew's Church on Park Avenue and asked him if he would hold a service on their premises.*

### Bill Tully—For JP Morgan Chase, we invented a form of interfaith worship.

For the service at JP Morgan Chase, we more or less invented a form of interfaith worship, Christian/Jewish/Muslim, that we felt had integrity and worked for those con-cerned. There were two big floors at the top of their building and they crowded people in. They also video linked the service to about 100,000 employees around the world. I was the officiating clergyman, but I had them get ten employees representing major tra-ditions within their company, each to do part of the prayers of the people. I did a talk and they did some music. But the extraordinary thing was—the people who planned the service told me that their employees really said, "We have got to do something." When I asked them, "To your knowledge, does anybody remember when you have ever done a prayer service on your turf during business hours?" They answered "No."

*Other corporations heard about that service. Some of them whose headquarters had been in the World Trade Center set up suites at the Waldorf Hotel, just a few blocks from St. Bartholomew's Church, where the CEOs could visit with employees or families of those who had been killed. So St. Bartholomew's became the locale for their services also.*

We held eight big memorial services at St. Bartholomew's for other companies that had lost people and needed a large church in midtown that was open to the notion of interfaith worship. The core of each service was three sections with Christian, Jewish and Muslim leaders. And each section had a reading, then a homily and a prayer from that tradition. So that rather than melding everything, each tradition was represented in its integrity. I don't want to tell you that even under these circumstances it was all sweetness and light, because for some people the idea of interfaith worship—everybody in the same room at the same time—was intolerable. Everybody was under strain. And there were some other touchy moments in the planning of these services, but I think that in the main, people were very comforted. In many cases, families would have had their own individual services, so this was the company trying to acknowledge what had happened.

What we, at St. Bart's, learned about how to do this and the relationships that we built with companies is something that I have been trying for years to do. I have tried to get an appointment with the chairman of some of these companies. In ordinary times, they don't see the importance of religious cooperation. They think some line is being crossed. Suddenly, in this event, a lot of this separation crumbled, and I think these will be lasting relationships between our world and the corporate world.

## ST. THOMAS CHURCH

*St. Thomas Church, Fifth Avenue, in Manhattan, was the location for another special service, one to commemorate all the people from the British Commonwealth who had perished in the disaster. The Rev. Harry Krauss, vicar of St. Thomas, described the initial request.*

### Harry Krauss—The Prime Minister is coming.

Some people from the Consul General's office came over to see me on Monday, September 17. I know it was Monday because the rector's off that day, otherwise they would have seen him. Ray Raymond, the political advisor to the Consul General, asked if we would be able to do a memorial service for the British community and outlined what he thought they'd like. When I said, sure, he said they'd like to have the service in two days. I checked with the rector, who supported the idea. So we said yes, we all smiled and shook hands and out the door they went. I switched into action to get the ball rolling.

Then they called back about an hour later and Ray said, "There's been a development, may we come back?" And, I said, "Can't we talk about this on the phone?" They said, "No, we've got to come back over to see you." Over they came, and when they got back in my office, they told us that the Prime Minister would be coming. And I said, "Well then we *are* talking about security." That of course really escalated the whole event—we had two days of three-ring-circusry.

*Planned to honor the more than two hundred people from every part of the British Commonwealth who lost their lives on 9/11, the service was scheduled to begin at 2:00 P.M. but was delayed almost an hour because the car carrying Prime Minister Tony Blair from the airport was tied up in traffic. When it finally began, the British Ambassador to the United States, Sir Christopher Meyer, read this letter from Her Royal Majesty, Queen Elizabeth.*

You come together today in St. Thomas Church in New York united in sorrow by the terrible events of last week. Each and every one of us has been shocked and numbed by what we have witnessed in these recent days.

But none of us should doubt the resilience and determination of this great and much loved city and its people. Men and women from many nations, from many faiths and from many backgrounds were working together in New York City when this unimaginable outrage overtook them all.

At your service today, we think especially of the British victims. For some of them, New York was simply a stopover on some busy travel schedule. For others it was a workplace of excitement and of opportunity. For many it was a familiar second home.

These are dark and harrowing times for families and friends of those who are missing or who suffered in the attack—many of you here today. My thoughts and my prayers are with you all now and in the difficult days ahead.

But nothing that can be said can begin to take away the anguish and the pain of these moments. Grief is the price we pay for love.

There was a reception afterwards at which the family members brought from Britain had the chance to meet Prime Minister and Mrs. Blair. Many other dignitaries were present: Mayor Rudolph Giuliani, Governor George Pataki, Secretary General Kofi Annan, former President William J. Clinton. The proceedings were broadcast live in the British Isles and for months afterwards, St. Thomas had a steady stream of visitors from Britain who had seen the service and wanted to worship in the church where it had been held.

## Harry Krauss—The British families were undone by the death of their relatives.

So many of the families who had come for the service were undone by the death of their relatives, but they were exceedingly gracious and astonished that we would do all this for them. That attitude was expressed again and again, that they were absolutely astonished that an American parish would do this kind of thing for them when obviously we must have had our own people involved in the tragedy.

*St. Thomas continued to serve as an important locale for British memorial activities. On October 14, when Prince Andrew visited New York City on behalf of Her Majesty the Queen, he also came to express her gratitude to St. Thomas Church. At the Sunday morning service, he read the Old Testament lesson and later met parishioners at the coffee hour before moving on to other official functions, including the reception announcing that Queen Elizabeth was bestowing an honorary knighthood on Mayor Rudolph Giuliani.*

*On September 10, 2002, the one-year anniversary, members of New York's British community gathered again, this time with the Archbishop of Canterbury George L. Carey, for a choral evensong and dedication of a memorial. St. Thomas' rector, the Rev. Andrew C. Meade, described the memorial.*

## Andrew Meade—Our grief echoes in the heart of God.

The memorial is the image of Christ Crucified, a 400-year-old figure, which has been attached to the Cross of Stones from Mount Calvary inlaid in the column next to the pulpit. It is given, as the inscription says, "In loving memory of David Dewey Alger and all who were killed in the terrorist attack on the World Trade Center, New York City, September 11, 2001." David Alger was an American and a lover of Britain and things British.

We asked and were graciously given permission by Her Majesty to use for this crucifixion memorial the final sentence of her message last year to the congregation at the special service here last September. We will cut those words in the stone, together with notice of today's dedication by Archbishop Carey, beneath what is already there for the memorial inscription. The Queen's words are, "Grief is the price we pay for love." When you associate that statement with the image of Christ on his cross, you realize that it is also a word about God. Grief is the price that God has paid for his love for the human race.

Our faith can lead us to see that Ground Zero is a similar spiritual place to the foot of the cross. The grief at both those places is connected, and it echoes in the heart of God.

## CATHEDRAL OF ST. JOHN THE DIVINE

*The St. Francis Day Service at the Cathedral of St. John the Divine traditionally celebrates the magnificence of God's creation. Using the music of Paul Winter's Earth Mass, the service includes the stately procession of creatures of every kind from small insects and fishes to larger and larger mammals and birds that are carried or led up the great aisle to the altar in the central crossing. People are encouraged to bring their pets with them to be blessed outside at the fair that follows the service.*

*Obviously, there were questions about whether this event should proceed on October 7, 2001 as planned. After much discussion, the cathedral staff decided that to place before the wounded city a vision of the goodness of God's creation might actually hasten the healing process. Asha Golliher, the coordinator of the afternoon's fair, provided one glimpse of such healing.*

### Asha Golliher—St. Francis Day Procession of Animals.

We wanted to be open especially to what people needed in the community and also do something very appropriate. Mary Bloom, who organizes the procession, invited some of the workers with the rescue dogs to be in the procession. I think we had as many as six rescue workers. Some of them were firemen and others were volunteers, a lot of the rescue dogs are in fact volunteered. They lined up in front of the church and people knew who they were. We didn't put them in the robes that we ordinarily put the animal leaders in. We left the rescue workers in their uniforms. When they came down the center aisle as part of the procession on St. Francis Day, it was so beautiful. People wept to see them and were so grateful for the opportunity to be with them in this way, in the sacred procession. The dogs, and the workers themselves, their trainers also wept to be so greeted. The church holds 4,000 people and people were standing and absolutely silent as they marched down the aisle and up to the altar. The animals were blessed by the bishop and the clergy at the altar.

Then they came to the fair. They had a station at the fair, on the driveway with other exhibiters, including the Society for the Prevention of Cruelty to Animals. The SPCA had a brand new veterinary van that they placed at Ground Zero to take care of the rescue animals, to nurture them and take care of their burned feet and give them water and food. All day long people came by to pet these animals. The dogs lay there and absorbed all of this love. The workers had pictures from their searches and told us stories of how depressed the animals had become at not being able to find live people in the wreckage, and how healing it was for them to be able to come to this service of blessing and to be so well received by the community.

## A Service of Remembrance, Reflection and Hope—October 16, 2001

*Fiduciary Trust Company was one of the firms with the highest percentage of casualties on 9/11. Their offices were located above the ninetieth floor of Tower Two, above the floors where the second plane hit. Of the employees who were already at work that day, only one man managed to escape; eighty-seven employees were killed. To honor those who had perished, the company held a "Service of Remembrance, Reflection and Hope" at the Cathedral of St. John the Divine on October 16, 2001. Over five thousand family-members, clients, and current employees attended the service. Vice-Chairman James C. Goodfellow, a parishioner from St. Mary's Church, Tuxedo Park, described the planning of the service.*

### James C. Goodfellow—Our employees were from many faiths.

I thought of St. John the Divine initially because it was clear that it welcomes every-body. It's not just an Episcopal church; it's a house of God. Having every religious group represented by the people we lost, having to come together as a family, then we had to come to some building that would welcome us, where we would not feel too directed toward one way or another. The service at St. John the Divine spoke to everybody. Everybody suffered. It wasn't *Episcopalians* that suffered, or *Jewish* people, it was *people* that suffered. They happen to believe different ways, but that's irrelevant. We came through this process together and that particular church welcomed us all together.

Our clients, too, were very much part of the grieving process, part of the hope. In many ways a portfolio manager becomes part of the family, working with you, your parents and your children as they manage your funds for you. When that life is snuffed out, someone who was like family, you grieve. Our clients attended that service in droves. They are our friends, like family.

## CHURCH OF OUR SAVIOR, CHINATOWN

*Some of the changes brought about by 9/11 were small. The Church of Our Savior in Chinatown had for some time opened its facilities after school so that children from the first to fourth grades could do their homework there. Children can use the books in the church library and a teacher is always present to help the students as they study. Most of the students who come are not Christian, but, as program director Peter Ng explained, "We think of ourselves as a church providing good soil for the community. We are not planting seeds, but we are providing good soil for the seeds—maybe they will grow eventually."*

### Peter Ng—Oh Peter, why?

A lot of children came to me and said, "Oh Peter, why? Why did the airplane have to hit the building? A lot of people died." They are very young; they didn't know.

I had to say, "In the world, there are angels and then there is the devil. But God is sending us a very strong message that you need to be a good person. Then if you are a good person, you will not do things like this, right? So remember, it's a very sad story. A lot of children lost their father or mother, but you are very fortunate because you still have your parents. So you have to be a good person when you grow up." I had a seminarian who was helping us with the outreach program. So I asked her to read a Bible story to the children. She comes now twice a week and has a Bible study for the children. The children like it and their parents feel that the church is a safe place for their children.

## PORT AUTHORITY OF NEW YORK AND NEW JERSEY

*The Port Authority lost eighty-four employees in the 9/11 disaster: officers who were responsible for the various systems within the World Trade Center, employees who worked in the Port Authority offices there and people involved in the train and tunnel systems. Because Port Authority personnel were so directly involved in the relief operations and because destroyed offices had to be reestablished in new locations, it was not until the six-month anniversary of the tragedy that the Port Authority held memorial services for those who had died. The Seamen's Church Institute was asked to assist in planning and presenting the services of remembrance which were held at the Brooklyn Terminal, at the New Jersey Marine Terminal and at the Seamen's Church Institute's Chapel on March 11, 2002. SCI chaplain Jacques Girard, a deacon in the Diocese of New York, talked about the service.*

### Jacques Girard—We did an ecumenical service together.

Our service was held at the Port Authority Building in Red Hook. Officiating were myself, representing Seamen's Church, and then there were the two Roman Catholic chaplains. We did an ecumenical service together for the Port Authority people who worked in that section of Brooklyn. There was a mix of white- and blue-collar workers. And it was quite full, about seventy people. It was for those that had died, for those that were working at Ground Zero, and the families. We had a many prayers covering a wide range of concerns.

# FAMILY ASSISTANCE CENTER

*Episcopal chaplains also served at the Family Assistance Center sponsored by the Red Cross and located first at Pier 94 and then later on Chambers Street. To work there one had to be certified as a chaplain by the Red Cross, a process that involved presenting your credentials and taking a brief training program. Sister Ellen Francis, an ordained priest who is also a member of the Order of St. Helena, was one of the chaplains who worked there each Thursday until the Center closed.*

### Ellen Francis—So I made up ID cards on the computer.

Of course, the Red Cross did ask for credentials. At St. Helena's we don't have an ID card, so I made up little ID cards on the computer for both of us with our pictures and got them laminated at Office Depot so they looked quite professional. We proudly showed our ID cards, which were immediately accepted. It's been very handy to have since then.

*In the early days, the Assistance Center dealt primarily with family members still caught up in the trauma of losing loved ones so the chaplains were busy with grief counseling.*

We had chaplains from all different faiths. There were Muslims and Jews and people from many different Christian denominations as well. We were serving people. There was a tremendous diversity in the people we were serving. We would always be there for those people with whatever questions they were asking, to listen to what they had to say, to support them in their faith in wherever they were with what had happened on that terrible day.

*One of the early responsibilities of the chaplains at the center was to accompany families on their first visit to Ground Zero. The families would assemble at Pier 94, be introduced to their chaplains, and then board a ferry that took them to the stop near the World Financial Center. Mary Ellen Blizzard, a laywoman from St. Luke in the Fields, was certified as a volunteer chaplain on September 14 and generally worked two days a week at the center throughout its existence.*

## Mary Ellen Blizzard—Those moments really stuck with me.

I think the most moving aspect of those trips was the people who were in roles other than being chaplains or mental health providers who were extraordinary in their reverence and care of the families. I remember this one ferry ride at the end of September when there was a black sheriff from New Jersey with us. When the ferry docked at the battery, he brought the families off the ferry very ceremoniously. He was walking backwards, swinging his arms, and leading them very reverently. It was so touching. I actually got to see him a few weeks later at the canteen, and I thanked him for what he had done. Those moments really stuck with me.

*As the intensive trauma counseling ended, the focus at the center shifted to dealing with more mundane issues of survival—finding new employment, housing, or relief assistance, and filling out the endless paperwork that was required of those who sought fed-*

*eral emergency aid. But through early March when the operation was phased out, chaplains continued to find long lines of people eager to talk to them.*

## Ellen Francis—This was a broad sweep of humanity.

For me, the most powerful thing of all was the walls—at the family center and also at the hospitals and various places around the city—walls with the pictures of people who were missing. It was so clear from those pictures that this was a broad sweep of humanity, people from all walks of life, from all parts of this world. The people we talked to had every kind of story, people's lives had been interrupted all of a sudden, without any warning. I can't give specifics, of course, because of confidentiality. But the number of loose ends and unfinished lives and unsaid feelings was tremendous. There were people who lost husbands, ex-husbands, children. One of the police officers there had found out after several weeks that two of his high school buddies were killed.

We also ministered to the volunteers. There were lawyers who volunteered to help with the death certificates. We also made a point of talking to the people who were serving in the booths to make sure they were taking care of themselves too, because many of them were not trained in any kind of pastoral ministry and were suddenly getting an overload of these tragic stories. That was a very important part of our work as well. The Red Cross itself was sending volunteers from all over the country for three-week shifts, for the most part, either mental health professionals or people who did all kinds of other jobs—purchasing, signing forms, food service, etc. So we kind of looked out for each other. Always the chaplains and health professionals worked together as a team to refer people back and forth.

The Red Cross did a good job of what they called debriefing or defusing. After each shift we would all meet with a chaplain and go around and talk about what had happened and say prayers for each other. So they really did pay attention to being sure that we were taking care of ourselves too. The last question was always, so what are you going to do for yourself today? That was always a good thing to remember, *always take care of you too.*

# CHAPLAINS AT GROUND ZERO

*The Rt. Rev. George Packard is the Episcopal Suffragan Bishop for Chaplaincies and serves as liaison to chaplains in the military and in other institutions such as hospitals and prisons. He was in his office at the National Church Center on 9/11, and immediately began to survey the ways in which chaplains would be called upon to cope with the tragedy. He went first to Bellevue Hospital, talked with several chaplains there, but gradually absorbed the fact that only very superficial casualties were coming in. The next day, as the magnitude of the disaster set in, Packard and his office team visited the Federal Emergency Management Agency command center, offered to be of service in managing chaplains on the site but found such chaos there that they left to explore the area around Ground Zero and meet with chaplains there.*

### George Packard—I never saw anything as awful as this in Vietnam.

I had been helping out at the field Morgue when someone asked me if I were a priest. I told him I was, but that I was not Roman Catholic. "I don't care," he said. And there was part of a body, it was adhered to an I-beam. It was awful. I mean, it was painfully awful to see this. And to see these wonderful firefighters, platoons of firefighters, rotate in and out of duty, and some of them didn't rotate, they stayed and milled around and got in each other's way. Noble, noble people. Wonderful people. But you did have those kinds of scenes, where guys were emotionally wired and would start to disassemble right there in the middle of the rescue and recovery area. That's why this 9/11 sort of rewrote the book when it came to critical incident stress. I was an officer in Vietnam. I'd never seen anything as awful as this. This was far and away the most brutal thing I've ever seen. It was awful.

*Later the Presiding Bishop and the Bishop of New York asked Bishop Packard to take charge of certifying and scheduling the Episcopal chaplains on the scene. He found a couple of FBI chaplains who were already on site who helped with the scheduling and*

*rotation and training of the chaplains. Together they made the necessary decisions—
How do you move chaplains into the site? What do you use as a staging area? What kind
of training do the chaplains need? How do you debrief them after their shifts?
Chaplains needed to be able to distinguish between post-traumatic stress (in people
who actually saw people dropping out of the building, for example) and critical incident
stress (in people directly involved in the recovery effort—police, firefighters, Con-Ed
technicians, EMS workers). Packard found a consulting psychologist in New Jersey,
David Knowlton, who set up a training program that was used in all the dioceses con-
tiguous to New York, Pennsylvania, Virginia and Washington, D.C. to train possible
chaplains. The office even produced a CD on Critical Incident Stress Management that
can be used in any diocese that is confronted with a massive tragedy.*

In a debriefing, you need to let people tell their story. For example, we did one session
in Washington, DC. There were some guys who were sitting there with arms folded,
almost saying "like you guys from New York, you're going to tell us what our pain is?"

But then, we played a videotape with some music, and they started to loosen up and
talk, and they wanted us to hear that their reaction to the tragedy at the Pentagon was one
of anxiety, not of depression. They kept remembering that one of those planes never
made it to its target. Where the hell was it going? See, there was a whole different dynam-
ic there. A number of priests made the mistake of being chaplains down at Ground Zero
on Saturday night and then going back into their parishes on Sunday. You don't want to
do that because all of that stuff starts to tumble out, unfiltered, unprocessed, and that's
not good. So our focus was to debrief the clergy as much as possible, so that they could
learn the skills and apply to them to themselves and their congregations.

*Packard assembled chaplaincy experts to take the crisis intervention-training pack-
age around the country. The team consisted of Francis Zanger, a chaplain and a specialist in trauma for submariners for the CIA; Mike Stewart, a specialist in trauma to
pediatric environments; Babs Meairs, a chaplain from the West Coast; Jackie Means, a
specialist in prison ministries who was the first woman ordained as priest after the
General Convention approved women's ordination. Some of the people on the team had
served at Ground Zero, others had not. "We also had a liturgical specialist," emphasized*

*Packard. "At the end of the day, Episcopalians translate what they do, their theology, into liturgy. Having a liturgist on the team was important to us."*

*One of the first such workshops was held in the Diocese of Newark.*

## Jack Croneberger—A tremendous help to our Diocese.

There were two days of workshops and he brought some fascinating people in who had tremendous skills. Some of them had dealt with national crisis and disaster situations, which they were able to translate into our more particular focus here. There was a lot of very positive feedback from both clergy and laity who participated.

*Many priests who took this training in various parts of the country, later came to minister at Ground Zero. To screen such volunteers, the chaplaincy office often sent them first to St. Paul's Chapel, "that gracious place of hospitality," said Packard. "I wanted it to be sort of a gentle filter where we might decide whether to allow those people to go on to Ground Zero. I think the toleration of the St. Paul's team was significant. They not only ministered to recovery workers, they ministered to volunteers and chaplains whom they'd see needed that ministry."*

*The Ground Zero chaplains worked in two-person teams on eight-hour shifts—three teams each twenty-four hours. They generally met their replacements at St. Paul's, and then spent most of the time walking around Ground Zero, being available to talk to workers or bystanders. Before the Morgue ministry was regularized, the roving chaplains would visit the Morgue or sometimes even be called into the Pit. Deacon Edgar Hopper of St. Augustine's Church on the Lower East Side of Manhattan described one such visit.*

## Edgar Hopper—There were cranes looking like praying mantis.

I checked in one night at about a quarter of twelve at the fire department command headquarters and told the chief there that I'd be walking north if he needed me. Before I could get around to the north side, he called me on the phone and said, "They need a chaplain at the north side." And so I said, "Okay, there are two of us." He said, "Send one on the west side of the hole, and one on the east, they're trying to find a body; they don't know which way they'll be able to bring it out."

So we went down in the hole, about fifteen to twenty feet. He was on east side; I was on the west side. And it was so Kafkaesque, you know? That smoke was rising. It was yellow. It was frightening. It had a lot of sulfur in it. Smoke was coming from around your boots and the like. Every time another part of the hole opened, fire would shoot out of it again. And there were these huge cranes looking like giant preying mantis, digging up and making holes. And there were lights. And there were ironworkers, with these huge acetylene torches cutting, and guys digging with what looked like little implements you would use on a patio window box. Then finally they were able to extricate this body.

So they put it in the body bag. They formed a line and they handed the stretcher up to the edge. And by this time the priest had come around; he was at the head and I was at the foot. And when I looked up there were about fifteen fire, police and EMS guys on either side, and we prayed. Somebody said it was an EMS guy. And I realized at that moment that could have been my son. Because he's an EMS worker (though I knew he was safe.) And I felt really grateful . . . and spiritually there was a reinforcement of the belief that God will send for you when He wants you.

And, in fact, the priest I was working with, he said to me, "I've got to go back." So we got one of the guys who had their little carts and he took us back to St. Paul's. And this priest, all he could say was, "Why can't men be kinder to each other?" He started to cry and shake, while I was trying to hold him.

*Packard's office continued to schedule chaplains for Ground Zero until mid-November, 2001, when that function was taken over entirely by the Red Cross. Episcopal chaplains then continued to serve at the Morgue until the clean-up operation closed in June 2002.*

# 5
## THE FUTURE

## PROMOTE PEACE

*Perhaps the most persistent theme from the people interviewed for this book is the determination to promote peace. Setting this theme, Presiding Bishop Frank Griswold's public statement on 9/11, ended with the words:*

May our response be to engage with all our hearts and minds and strength in God's project of transforming the world into a garden, a place of peace where swords can become plowshares and spears are changed into pruning hooks.

*Archbishop Rowan Williams echoed this theme in his September 12 address to the clergy.*

**Rowan Williams—I wouldn't want what we experienced to happen to anyone.**

Suffering humiliates us and we want to make a difference. We want it to be otherwise. And one of the ways in which we try to make it otherwise is to do something that may not resolve the situation, but releases our tensions. I'm sure that in the city and the country in the days ahead, the pressure to do something, anything, is going to be greater and greater. The rhetoric will become more and more intense. One thing I want to say to that is a very simple personal observation which I found coming out this morning when I was asked about this by a journalist from the United Kingdom. Quite simply: I wouldn't want that to happen to anybody. And sometimes those very elementary Ethics 101 responses are the important ones. I wouldn't want that to happen to anyone. I wouldn't want to see another room of preschool children being hurried out of a building, under threat. I wouldn't want to see thousands of corpses given over for the justification of some principle. And very simply: I don't want anybody to feel what others and I were feeling at about 10:30 yesterday morning. I've been there.

*Even Bishop George Packard, who serves the U.S. Armed Forces as Bishop, agreed that war was not the answer.*

## George Packard—We ought to be able to wage reconciliation.

I do not think taking this war into Afghanistan, and pounding the rubble, and making us feel good as we pinpoint bomb Al-Quaeda is any kind of an answer to this pain. I think we need to be able to have enough courage to stand in the vulnerability that these kinds of events bring before us. Just as we seem to have so much resource to wage revenge, we ought to be able to wage reconciliation. As Presiding Bishop Frank Griswold says, "We are to be the healers of the world." That's what we do. That's our commission.

*Phil Brochard was in his second year at General Theological Seminary when the towers fell. Talking two years later, he explained what that experience had done to his own sense of vocation.*

## Phil Brochard—9/11 changed how I viewed being a Christian.

I was pretty sure when I came to seminary that I wanted to be a priest. I mean, I don't know how entirely sure you can be to do this vocation. But 9/11 really changed how I viewed being a Christian. I'd always considered my Christianity to be something that was integral to my life but that didn't separate me that much from others. The events of 9/11 really tested what a Christian vocation in this life is, and what it is to be a Christian in America specifically, in response to the rhetoric of vengeance and hate that came in the days following.

It also made it very difficult for me as a person who lived in New York and who saw what had gone down two miles away and had friends that were providing the pastoral support down at the Ground Zero morgue. To see all that made it very difficult for me as a Christian to come from a place of vengeance and hate and revenge. So it really solidified a lot of what I had been thinking, talking and writing about—a pretty firm vocation and calling for peace.

It's plain that I must talk about the Prince of Peace in this world. What is different is how people respond to that message now. I think more people are aware of a reality that's not centered on violence. Delivering that message is not always easy. And it's not always easy to hear, especially when people in the mainstream really want leadership that is asking for war and for vengeance and for preemptive strikes and things of that nature. But I think that's what we have to preach. That Christ didn't take up a sword to get retribution, he gave himself up. And as Christians our witness is to do that. Our witness is to bear that violence and give love in return. That's something that's not easy.

People talk about peace all the time as if it was a non-active response, as if it was an easy thing to do. And there is nothing easy about peace. When you're being attacked, when the violence is coming to you, true peace is to be able to respond in love. And we'll always have an opportunity for that.

*On 9/11, Jeremy Lucas and his wife, Penny, had just arrived at General Theological Seminary from Alabama, to begin his first year as a theological student.*

## Jeremy Lucas—I knew that this would change the type of priest I would be.

I knew immediately that this would change the type of person, the type of Christian, the type of priest that I would be forever. Nearly a year from the events of 9/11, a group of us here decided that we wanted to look at how Christians, and how specifically our church, responded and was going to continue to respond in a peaceful and non-violent way. We formed a chapter here of the Episcopal Peace Fellowship. My vision for this group is for us to look creatively at peaceful responses and peace and justice issues, in order that we would not be so stuck on those knee-jerk reactions that we seem to have about issues around violence and conflict.

I think that seminaries are a place where people who are specifically studying to go out into the world as priests can do creative, new thinking prayerfully, with reflection on Scripture. With the faculty and students involved here, a lot of new thought could come out of this group. We need to learn to walk on that line that says if I am faithful and this is true, what is my response? Where do I go from here?

I think probably the biggest inspiration that I have gotten is from a group called 9/11 Families for Peaceful Tomorrows, a group of people who lost loved ones in the attacks who have decided that their reaction is not going to be revenge, is not going to be "we have to get those people." It is "How can we keep this from happening again? How can we show a loving response in the face of such terror?" For me, watching people who actually lost loved ones say those words is incredible.

*As its first major project, the seminary's Episcopal Peace Fellowship chapter sponsored "From Violence to Wholeness," a three-day seminar directed toward nonviolent personal, interpersonal and social transformation. The seminar was open to visitors as well as the seminary community. So many other people had similar sentiments.*

*Dean Ward Ewing addressed the seminary community on September 14, 2001.*

## Ward Ewing—Killing 10,000 people of Arab descent will not heal our loss.

We must seek justice; we must seek to do all we can to end terrorism. But we must do so in a way that will lead to the reduction of violence, not it's increase. Killing 10,000 innocent people of Arab descent will not heal our loss, but it will give victory to those who propound the use of violence. We are called to be peacemakers. Making peace always includes taking upon oneself the suffering of others.

First we need to grieve, to weep, lest our sorrow turn to bitterness.

Then we need to make a response, fueled by the desire for peace, not the anger of hatred. We are in a war—but it is not a war between the U.S. and Arab states. It is a war between the forces of evil and the forces of good. It is fought within our hearts. It is fought within our social structures. And it is fought within our world. To return increased violence for violence will give the victory to the forces of evil. The way of victory is a way of forgiveness, justice, mercy, collaboration, due process, unity—the way of peace.

*Joan Quilter is a senior citizen who lives at St. Margaret's House. As a grandmother who lived through the German bombing of London in World War II, she compared her experience on 9/11 to that time.*

## Joan Quilter—I'd like to see my granddaughters grow up and be happy.

A lot of residents have been through experiences, maybe not as bad as this, but unfortunately as you get older it's part of life. But then you have to look for the good side. Good things happened here after 9/11. I loved seeing the children play. That was a lovely thing. You feel there's hope and there's youth and hopefully, we will have peace. I know most of the grownups are praying for peace. Also, that we can have peace for the children and that they can grow up in peace. That's my wish anyway, because I have grandchildren, two granddaughters, and I'd like to see them grow up and be happy.

## Mike Kendall—The theology of war is bankrupt.

I can't imagine why anybody would want to ever support a war. I think what Jesus teaches is absolutely the only way. I always believed it—I know it now. I cannot imagine inflicting that horror on anybody. That's why I'm so absolutely opposed to war and to the bombing in Iraq. It's wrong. So I think theologically, for a person like myself, the theology of war is bankrupt.

*The Rev Chloe Breyer went through cycles of hope and then disillusionment after the experience of 9/11.*

## Chloe Breyer—Then I went through a time of being very, very disillusioned.

I did have great hope for awhile that this would not only break down barriers between people in New York, but also between people in the U.S. and our fellow nations with which we share the planet. And then, that not clearly being the case, I think it was about the time of the "Axis of Evil" speech when suddenly I felt like, well what is all this? We have this huge amount of sacrifice and pain and it is for nothing because clearly we haven't learned that much. Then I went through a time of being very, very disillusioned, I think for quite a while, until I ran into these 9/11 Families for Peaceful Tomorrows.

# 9/11 FAMILIES FOR PEACEFUL TOMORROWS

*One unusual group that emerged is made up of family members of persons who died at the World Trade Center, in Pennsylvania and at the Pentagon. The 9/11 Families for Peaceful Tomorrows, as it is called, has launched a major campaign to promote reconciliation rather than retaliation. The group had its genesis in late November 2001, when several family members walked from the Pentagon to Ground Zero, using that physical exercise as a means to work out the emotional chaos into which they had been plunged. The walkers were greeted at St. Francis Xavier Church in New York City by others who had not made the trip. At that evening's gathering, the overwhelming sentiment was that the military retaliation taking place in Afghanistan was the wrong course of action. A small group formed to lay plans for a peaceful response.*

*In January 2002, Global Exchange arranged a trip for some family members to visit Afghanistan, to meet with people who had lost loved ones there, visit hospitals and schools and see first hand the devastation there. On Valentine's Day, the organization was formally launched with a press conference and a website. By the end of 2002, over sixty family members and about 1,000 supporters had joined the group.*

*Colleen Kelly is one spokesperson for the group. She is a young nurse practitioner, mother of three, from the Bronx, whose brother, William, died at the World Trade Center.*

We do a lot of interfaith work. It started off as a very natural thing because we were invited to speak very often in churches and mosques. We have a strong commitment to recognizing the difference between Islamic terrorists and the religion of Islam. That is very, very important. Our group itself is incredibly interfaith. Though I am Catholic, there are atheists, Jews, Christians, Muslims, agnostics, and Buddhists. We're a secular group made up of people who come from very different religious backgrounds.

We have a two-fold mission. The first is to seek out all effective alternative responses to acts of terrorism, alternatives other than violence or militarism. Our great hope is to begin to cultivate that discussion in an in-depth way. And our second mission is with families around the world. For me this whole notion of what it would mean to respond and to reconcile non-violently, that's the essence of my faith. Who better to be speaking out about this than victims of violence?

For me the idea of prayer and knowing that we really can't do this alone is a huge notion. It's really comforting to me to think that God is here with us, especially that certainly God was with my brother on that day. The whole idea of the crucifixion—the suffering on the cross—has become enormously deep in my life. Having Jesus not only become human but also choosing to suffer the way he did. I think for me that was never so concrete as it became on 9/11, knowing that those hours on the cross were the same as the hours that my brother was really suffering.

*Members of the 9/11 Families for Peaceful Tomorrows have contributed to the rebuilding of the Mosque in Afghanistan and have worked in conjunction with a number of the interfaith initiatives of the Diocese of New York.*

# EPISCOPAL-MUSLIM RELATIONS

*A major area of concern brought into sharp focus by the events of 9/11 was the question of Christian-Muslim relations. As people learned that the attack had been designed and executed by a dedicated group of Muslim terrorists, acts of terrorism against Muslims in New York escalated and many Muslim citizens feared for their lives. However, this climate of suspicion and fear also challenged Christians to rethink the implications of a gospel that called for love rather than hate and demanded understanding rather than prejudice.*

*The Diocese of New York was fortunate to have a group of people who had been working to facilitate Christian-Muslim understanding. Formed a decade ago during the Gulf War and called the Diocesan Episcopal-Muslim Relations Committee (EMRC), it was chaired by Lucinda Mosher, a graduate student at General Theological Seminary writing her dissertation on the moral vision of Islam. Members of that committee had a wide expertise in the faith and practice of Islam and together the committee had developed connections with many Muslim leaders. Thus, a basis for interfaith conversations had already been established and would prove very useful after 9/11 when many congregations began to seek a deeper understanding of Islam.*

*In the immediate aftermath of the attack, the first concern was for the safety of Muslim friends. One worried person was the Rev. Masud Syedullah, priest-in-charge of the Church of the Atonement in the Bronx, who had been raised by a Muslim father and Christian mother.*

## Masud Syedullah—My friends were hiding out.

I was concerned with the safety of Muslims in this country, fearing backlash. Directly across the street from me, there are three houses of Palestinians, longtime friends of mine. I noticed that they were not around. I didn't see them. They're usually out on the street. The women take the children to school in the morning, and they usually congregate outside the house afterwards. The men often congregate on the street after hours in the evening, talking and such. But I didn't see anybody. No one was around. I waited a couple of days, and then I e-mailed them. And sure enough, I discovered that they were there, but they were afraid. One of the young men, a student at City College, hadn't been to classes in three days. They were literally hiding out.

I also contacted the Bronx Muslim Center to see how things were going with them, and what was happening there. They had had threats left on the answering service and things like that. But no one was actually beaten up or killed. So Father Joel Mason, from St. Mary's Church, Chappaqua, and I interviewed them for an article in *The Episcopal New Yorker* that was printed in the November/December edition of 2001. The article's purpose was both to interview them about their experiences post 9/11 and to help educate Episcopalians in this diocese about Islam.

*In the ensuing months, the Diocesan Episcopal-Muslim Relations Committee worked on two major projects. One was a forum—part of the cathedral's Forums on Religion and Public Life—on "Fundamentalism in Islam, Judaism and Christianity." On November 17, 2001, 250 religious leaders from New York City gathered at the Cathedral of St. John the Divine for a dialogue led by Karen Armstrong, author of* A History of God, *a book about Islam; Dr. Susannah Heschel, Professor of Jewish studies at Dartmouth; Feisal Abdul Rauf, Imam of the al-Farah Mosque in New York City; and Jim Wallace, editor-in-chief of* Sojourners *magazine. These speakers brought great expertise and wisdom to the subject of interfaith relationships and charged the audience with the task of learning more about each other's beliefs and activities. With the help of Trinity Church, the event was filmed and downlinked to many communities throughout the United States.*

*The Rev. Stephen Holton, rector of St. Paul's Episcopal Church in Ossining, New York, described the genesis of the second project, to rebuild a mosque in Afghanistan. Because his father was in the diplomatic corps, Holton had lived in many parts of the world, and his enthusiasm about the richness that people of other cultures brought to his life led to his helping to form the Episcopal-Muslim Relations Committee in the 1990s.*

## Stephen Holton—Rebuilding the mosque would bring innocent people together.

About the fourth day into the bombing campaign, Bishop Sisk heard on the radio that a mosque north of Kabul had been destroyed. And he walked into a meeting of the Episcopal-Muslims Relations Committee, and said, "Wouldn't it be wonderful if the Diocese of New York helped to rebuild this mosque in a Ground Zero to Ground Zero relationship?" So many buildings had been destroyed. So many people had been killed in both New York City and Afghanistan. There were two groups of people, two sets of worshipers who were tragically hurt as a result of all of this violence. We thought that rebuilding the mosque would be a way for innocent religious people of both sides to come together.

*The committee members endorsed the project enthusiastically and immediately found others willing to help. An international organization called Global Exchange located the mosque and arranged a trip to survey the damage there. Funds came in from as far away as the Diocese of California where the Rt. Rev. William Swing has been working for years to promote interfaith action projects. Imam Mohammad Sherzad of the Masjid Hazrat-I-AbuBaker Sadiq in Flushing, a mosque whose congregation included many immigrants who had fled Afghanistan during the civil war, wanted to help raise the funds.*

## Mohammad Sherzad—Building a mosque is an act of prayer.

When I went back to Afghanistan, I found that the Taliban had told the people that the Afghanis who left for the West had separated themselves from God and were no longer following the ways of Islam. So my people here were very eager to help, and this idea of two faiths working together was very new to them and also very pleasant. The Qu'ran says that the building of a mosque is an act of prayer.

## Stephen Holton—You can actually build peace!

I've been writing to various people, and all I can call it is, building peace, stone by stone. You can actually build peace! And what a very wonderful thing it will be to show Muslims and Christians of America together with Muslims of Afghanistan dedicating this new house of God that we built together. That absolutely is an act of prayer that will have many fruits.

*Holton is clear about the impact of Muslim-Christian dialogue on his own life. He described learning about hospitality when he was in Afghanistan to see the bombed mosque.*

A number of us on the delegation were in a small, poor village on the edge of Kabul. We were visiting a man who had lost his home in the coalition bombing and his children had died. A very peaceful man, he invited us into his home. It was made up of a very small outer room, a place to put shoes, and there was a stove there. And then an inner room that was probably about ten feet square or something like that, with a carpet on the floor and cushions around the edge and we were all sitting around. At a certain point he disappeared and then he reappeared with a tray with glasses of tea and some sweets on it. And we all shared tea. At that moment there was peace in a complete religious sense. And that's where I learned that all it takes is tea, all it takes is hospitality, to transform a meeting into a religious experience. This poor man understood that you actually don't need very much to offer hospitality.

*The funds necessary to rebuild the mosque were raised; a local construction crew completed the work and in February 2003, Stephen Holton represented the Diocese of New York at the dedication of the new building.*

## Stephen Holton—Thank you for having me, Afghanistan.

We go in. Two hundred people are there from the village. The county supervisor is there, a very distinguished and kind man. Bishop Sisk's letter is presented, with translation. Both the original and the Dari will be hung in the mosque.

I speak. I speak of having been there before, and the work we have done together, of 9/11 and the bombing of their mosque, about the need for holy space in time of war so we can rebuild our lives, about reconciliation and the need for all the children of Abraham to do God's work of peace in the world. As I speak it is as if a way opens before my feet and I keep speaking. And the Way is Christ, and I follow the Way.

Connie, my trip partner, rises. She presents the Imam with a rock from the World Trade Center. He treasures it, turning it over and over. She speaks of hope rising from the rubble. The Imam gets up. He says that I had promised we would build this mosque last June. And now it is complete. This is the same young Imam who last June yelled at me for the American bombing and for making promises that were never kept.

Promises made, promises kept.

Mosque elders rise to thank Bishop Sisk and me for the mosque. They say I am always welcome, whenever I come back. We leave, after presenting them with mittens made by the women of my parish for the children of their mosque.

Driving through Istalif, the ruined resort village I saw last June, I see so many signs of life. Children are walking down the street. The street has neither potholes nor huge rocks in it. There is still much work to be done, shops to be rebuilt after the Taliban destroyed them, but so much rebuilding is already done. Cream-colored school buildings replace the UNICEF school tents.

I think I will be leaving tomorrow. I remember that as a child my mother told me that when I left a playmates' house after playing all day, I should seek out the hostess of the house and say: "Thank you for having me."

Thank you for having me, Afghanistan.

*Another member of the EMRC, Sister Ellen Francis of the Order of St. Helena, went with a women's delegation to Afghanistan in March 2003, to meet with Afghan women involved in education and government and to visit special programs for women such as crafts workshops, health facilities and widow's shelters. She continues to be a resource within the diocese to speak of the plight of Afghan women.*

# SEMINARY COURSES ON MUSLIM-CHRISTIAN UNDERSTANDING

*In another attempt to increase Muslim-Christian understanding, General Theological Seminary offered a course, An Anglican Response to Islam, for students at the summer continuing education program. Taught by the EMRC chair, Lucinda Mosher and the Rev. Dr. Bert Breiner, the course explored Anglican documents about Islam and Christian-Muslim relations that had been developed for various Lambeth Conferences. Students were laity and clergy from many parts of the United States. Professor Briener's lectures for the class were taped and the committee plans to put them together in a booklet to make them available to other parish study groups. The upsurge in parishes that want to offer study groups on Islam has kept EMRC members on high demand as speakers and resource people.*

*A similar course, taught by Mosher was repeated in the fall of 2002 for seminary students. The course included several visits to different Muslim communities, giving students the opportunity to experience the diversity within Islam itself. That course was part of what Mosher sees as EMRC's ongoing work.*

## Lucinda Mosher—That attack does not represent the Islam I know through my neighbor.

Quite honestly, while I'm happy to go out and talk to any parish anytime, you can't learn Christian-Muslim relations in a moment. Either you'll listen politely and leave with your same prejudices or you might get totally confused. It's important to have those events but that's not the way we're really going to understand each other fully. What we, as a committee, are trying to do is figure out how we can facilitate relationships that will be ongoing. We need to know what else would help. And what will the next need be? How can we be ready? We want to have more and more people able to say, "That attack was an aberration, it does not represent the Islam that I know through my neighbor."

*Independent of EMRC's work, another initiative grew in Westchester County. The Rev. Charles Colwell, rector of St. Barnabas Church in Irvington, described what happened.*

## Charles Colwell—I'm standing in solidarity with you.

On September 12, Julia de Peyster, a parishioner—a young mother—called me, saying, "I have just called the Westchester Rockland Islamic Center because I've heard some dreadful things that are happening in Westchester where people have been throwing things at Muslims and attacking them verbally. I told them I want you know I'm an Episcopalian from St. Barnabas Church in Irvington, and I'm standing in solidarity with you and will be praying for you on Sunday." I thought, "That's astounding! I didn't even think to do such a thing." And the more I thought about it, I thought we needed to do more.

So I called the mosque in Mount Vernon and asked the president of the mosque if he could find us a speaker to come to the church and participate in one of our Sunday morning services so that we could get to know more about Islam. I asked if other members of the mosque would be willing to come and stay for the coffee hour so that we could meet Muslims face to face, as opposed to reading about Islam in a book.

*Dr. Mahjabeen Hassan is a plastic surgeon in Westchester County and an active member of the mosque. She was identified as a person who might be willing to speak at the St. Barnabas service.*

## Mahjabeen Hassan—And you would give me your pulpit?

When Rev. Colwell called me, I had to ask him what he would you like to know about Islam. And the honesty which was there was incredible. He said, "I really don't know anything about Islam." And I thought, "You know where you are, then at least we can go forward." And to give me your pulpit to me, a pulpit is such a personal thing for everybody and their church. To give it to a Muslim to talk to the congregation on a Sunday, that was really honorable for my community and me. So, when I spoke that day, and the church was literally packed, it was very touching. It was like I was reading portions of Qur'an that were coming back to me, saying, "Yes, these are your cousins, except that you did not know them."

## Charles Colwell—It was an electric occasion.

They came, on the September 30. Thirty Muslims came—women with their head-dresses on, many doctors and professors. It was an electric occasion. A young man intoned prayers in Arabic at the beginning, at the middle and the end of the service, and they were translated immediately into English. And then Dr. Hassan spoke. She was dynamite. She explained basic Islam and her understanding of the differences between Islam and Christianity. And at the coffee hour afterwards, the chemistry was right. The two groups really met. We met each other, we got into deep dialogue with each other. And in that discussion it was one of the Muslim doctors who suggested that we include Jews in a continuing dialogue, which was wonderful.

*The next event held was a Day of Understanding on February 10 with a panel discussion exploring the commonalities of the three Abrahamic faiths, led by a Jewish Rabbi. From this meeting, the group went on to found the Center for Jewish-Christian-Muslim Understanding. Cherie Gaines, a retired lawyer who had been head of legal services at Bedford-Stuyvesant in Brooklyn, has been hired as the executive director of the center. Some of the funding has come from a St. Barnabas parishioner, Wright Salisbury, who lost his son-in-law on American flight 11 and was convinced of the necessity of interfaith understanding. Future plans include a festival for young people—Jewish, Islamic and Christian youths coming together at the synagogue on Sukkoth in the middle of September to have a pizza party under the Sukkoth booth so that they can meet socially and learn more about each other.*

## Charles Colwell—It's another thing to meet people face to face.

It's one thing to read books about other religions, it's another thing to meet people face to face and begin to feel a common humanity. I think all you have to do is look at 9/11 and look at the peril that we're in as a civilization, not only Americans but civilization itself. We're now able to destroy ourselves. We've always looked at other countries such as Northern Ireland or Israel and said, "It's too bad, they have terrible dangers there and terrorism but thank goodness it's somewhere else." We can't say that anymore. There's something very visceral about the fear that we've all experienced. And that brings us together on a level that unites us in a way that helps to break down some of the barriers and exclusive positions that we've taken in the past. To say that I have a corner on the truth, that's a very dangerous thing to say.

My relationship with God is soaring! I've gone deeper, and I've been fed in the last year by being more open. I feel God is moving me in a different way than in the past. I feel much more attuned and passionate about humanity than I did. It's the planet and it's civilization that we need to worry about. The world is such a tiny place, and our country has become such a pluralistic society. I have come to believe that God is in the midst of our pluralism. We can either make it work or not. And God wants us to make it work, and we have an opportunity here, a challenge that is so exciting. That's why I'm excited about the Center for Jewish-Christian-Muslim Understanding. We can do something as an organization to bring these faiths together that can help promote what God is doing in a unique way in the United States. There's a lot we can do right here in this country within our own spheres of influence to break down barriers and to get to know each other, respect each other and in many cases, love each other. And that's rich, but it's also imperative that we do it. It's not a luxury.

# SHARE THE STORY

### National Youth Event—Laramie, Wyoming

*In late July, 2002, young people and their advisors from across the United States gathered in Laramie, Wyoming, for the triennial Episcopal Youth Event. Along with the worship services and business meetings, the program included several workshops in which young people could share experiences and programs. The delegations from the Dioceses of New York and Long Island presented two workshops: one on the HIV-AIDS pandemic as it affects young people and one on the aftermath of 9/11. Brian Bing from Pearl River, New York, and Lily Acunzo from Staten Island, were among those who planned and presented the workshop.*

### Brian Bing—We didn't want people to be so apathetic to something as big as this.

We aimed the seminar to be personalized, because everyone had heard what had happened on the news. We had talked to people beforehand, asking, "What do you think about 9/11?" And we got answers like, "I'm from Seattle, it's across the country, it doesn't affect me." So that's what we really wanted to change, we didn't want people to be so apathetic to something as big as this, you know? And so we had the different teams from the Diocese of New York and the Diocese of Long Island come up, and we had about three or four stories, and I mean, there were some pretty heavy stories, some of them, and we had that happen. And the Diocese of Long Island provided a slide show, a Power Point presentation for us. It was a bunch of still shots, accompanied by classical music. They were divided into sections. The first was the destruction, what actually happened that day. And then the second was something I think everyone could relate to, and that was the worldwide response to what happened. And they had pictures from so many countries around the world, you know—Germany, Japan, England, France, everywhere—

putting flowers outside the United States Embassy, or holding candlelight vigils, and it was very comforting to know that the rest of the world was there with us.

## Lily Acunzo—I got really upset.

When we were preparing to do the hot topic, I got really upset, and I broke down. It was awful, I felt terrible. And I think that really reflecting on it kind of, it made it seem so much more real that way, you know? I remembered exactly where I was when I heard about it, and I got really upset and I didn't even know why I got so upset. And I think doing this whole seminar really gave me closure. It really, really gave me a sense of "It's done. I'm over it."

## Brian Bing—Everyone understands.

I think that was a really important part. Because when we first brought it up, it was an old topic to people. But as we got farther and farther into it, people were breaking down. People started to hate the fact that they were doing this, they hated doing work on it, because they didn't want to evoke these emotions, they didn't want to acknowledge that this happened. And at the end, when we were in the seminar room in the University of Wyoming, and there were about 150 kids in the room and they were all sitting there crying with us, that really put closure on it. We're not the only ones here, everyone understands.

## Lily Acunzo—Afterwards we had a giant hugging session.

Afterwards everybody in the room came up and a gave us all hugs. That was really fun. One person stood up and said, "It's amazing what you guys went through, and it's amazing that you're even here to talk about it and you're okay with it." And it was so great to know that all of these people in the room were feeling the same way I was, and were supportive of all of us, who were so close to it and everything. Even though they lived all over the United States. It was amazing feeling that unity.

## Brian Bing—Where was God on 9/11?

I think the best question someone asked me was, "Where was God on 9/11?" And I sat there and I…I really thought about it, and then I said, "Well I think that God actually did a lot despite what happened. There are acts of hate that are so strong that even God can do nothing to stop the actual act, but he made countless people late to work. Thank God only four thousand people died. I think the Twin Towers can hold fifty thousand people or something? And you know, people were late to work. My friend John had looked at some of the blueprints for the Twin Towers and said that at the angle it was hit, it should have come down a lot quicker than it really did, so a lot of people were actually able to get out. A lot of people were saved from the wreck. A lot of the fire fighters got up there, they saved the people, and they came down. That's where God was on 9/11."

*The George Packard, the Suffragan Bishop for Chaplaincies, was part of the staff from the Episcopal Church Center who came to Laramie for the youth event. He found himself very moved by the presentation.*

## George Packard—These youngsters had absorbed this crisis like a sponge.

Young delegates from Long Island and New York told their stories. And I had to listen because I wasn't even part of the program. I thought to myself, one of the reasons that the stories were so powerful and fresh was that these youngsters had absorbed this like a sponge. This was the trauma of their age. And then they, unlike the adults who kind of busied themselves doing all kinds of things that put this in a context, they felt helpless and could not do anything. That's the kind of thing that needs a debriefing. As Paul says, through hardship we have endurance and through endurance, we have character, and through character we have hope.

## One boy who lost his father.

*For one particular group of young people, those who lost parents in the attack, the road to healing is much more difficult. A teacher, who had been a part of the recovery crew the first week at Ground Zero, now counsels one such boy whose father was killed in the collapse of the towers.*

He's still very, very angry. And I think he is also angry because he wonders if anyone really cares that it was *his father* who died. Or whether people only care that it's a national tragedy—whether they're being patriotic rather than being interested in his individual mourning. He stays involved with the church and is looking for comfort but he doesn't want people to come out of the blue and say, "I know what you're going through." He wants a place where he can feel comfortable, but he doesn't trust the comfort that he gets from everyone because he thinks it's false.

I think that because this event is so huge, he doesn't want to be accused of making excuses for acting in a certain way because of the death of a dad. I don't understand his response to God, as such, but I do understand his response to God's people on earth as not wanting to feel like he's asking for help. It's a very adolescent male response that he's not supposed to cry, he's not supposed to ask for help, and that fear and sadness comes out as anger.

I'm trying to forget how useful I felt as a minister at Ground Zero and relate to this young man on the level of great tragedy, great questioning and great loss. We in the church should be ashamed that we got carried away with that event—the triumph over evil, triumph of God and the Holy Spirit. We should be terribly ashamed of ourselves because it's not a parade! It's not a cheer! It's much more serious than that. We're dealing with over two thousand people who lost fathers, mothers, brothers and sisters. So with this person, I try to knock all of that out. I try to say, "Okay, 9/11 was a great tragedy and because of that, you have a hard time trusting people who want to help you with your grieving. Give me a chance to prove I'm trustworthy and let's deal with your grieving. Let's deal with the fact that you lost a father, not that you lost a father in the largest event of terrorism on American soil." Because that doesn't matter to him. Nor should it. He lost a father. Whether his father died of a heart attack or got murdered, or got hit by a car, or was obliterated in the top of the World Trade Center doesn't matter.

*For many people, their first response to the news of 9/11 was one of prayer.*

## Linda Hanick—Reading the profiles became an act of prayer.

One of the projects I undertook right after 9/11 was to read every single profile in the *New York Times* of a person who had died. And the reason I did that is when I saw the second plane go in, I felt a lot of people had died, I wanted to know who they were. I wanted to have a connection to those people. And so, reading their profiles became an act of prayer, of thinking of the loved ones behind that person's life who were struggling with the question of where was God and basically praying that they would see God as they move forward in the future.

*A group from Christ Church, Bronxville, wanted to move beyond individual prayers to a corporate expression of concern. The church had an established a Center for Spiritual Growth that presented various programs to deepen the congregation's spiritual life so there was a cluster of people who had participated in such programs. The Center was directed by Hondi Brasco.*

## Hondi Brasco—Great joy and lots of consolation.

I put out an invitation to the community to ask who would like to come together in prayerful conversation about 9/11. A large number of women from Bronxville and the surrounding area met. We talked about 9/11. We talked through some of our grief, we talked about how we were praying about this. We met for about four weeks; it was a very large group from various churches, primarily a Christian group at that point. A core group of these women felt that we weren't finished after a month. We went on and it became a more ecumenical community, we had a Jewish member at one point, we had a Muslim woman join us and a Buddhist woman. We really began to pray together about the very difficult events that we were facing, including, of course 9/11 and the anthrax problem, and the death of Daniel Pearl, and the blow-up in the Middle East. It was very difficult to look at all those issues, but we discovered in our prayer community this ability to take our collective concern and anxiety and open it to prayer. We really had a sense of being led. We, as a community, found a great deal of joy, surprisingly enough, in terrible times and lots of consolation and we learned a lot from each other.

*The group had no agenda. At the beginning, Brasco would set questions like, "How are you praying about this?" "What would you tell your grandchildren about your thoughts at this time?" But gradually the group developed its own center and common concerns emerged spontaneously.*

My gut reaction to 9/11 was "What can we do to counter terrorism?" My thought was well "Let's have ten circles of light for every terrorist cell in the world." There may be 60,000 cells, but there are many, many more communities of light. Of course that does not mean denying our own darkness. A lot of the discussion was about "Why do they hate us?" There was a lot of self-searching about values, about what it means to be an American and how we might be perceived by others and questions about forgiveness. We are, I think as a community, exploring all of that.

We meet in a circle. And the center's empty. But it's also full of God's presence. I believe that we can stand around that emptiness, the Ground Zero of the heart, and trust that God is really present. I've felt that many times in the group. We were standing in prayer the other day, holding hands, and I thought, "That's right. That's what we do. We hold space. We hold this together. And then God does work. God is there in the most empty places." But I think the danger is in rushing to fill the space and losing that God connection. We want to remember and we want to stand with all who have lost someone, and we want also to stand for the new life that's possible.

At the end of our time together, we pray. We have listened to what was offered. We hold hands around that space. And we pray together. It's the evolution of an organic liturgy. It started with conversation. But it's become much more prayerful. I think that's what sustained us. I cannot speak highly enough for prayerful communities. What happened to us was a corporate, a collective tragedy, and, I think, in order to heal, we need a corporate, collective response. Much of what we have seen in spiritual direction has been focused on a personal journey. Although that is a very good thing, sometimes we're not always aware of the whole and of the role of community in terms of our spiritual journey. So, my experience suggests to me that we need to expand the circle, expand the circle of loving and do this together in some way.

# COPING WITH POST TRAUMATIC STRESS

*For many of the people who fled from the Twin Towers or watched the buildings collapse or worked frantically to clear away rubble, the trauma of 9/11 continues. Captain Jay Jonas, the fireman whose company survived the collapse of Tower One, admits he is still having a hard time.*

### Jay Jonas—There's a lot of baggage starting to come out.

For us, this is not over. People are very surprised to hear that. They say, "Well, it's been months. You should be over this by now." And for a lot of us, it's starting to manifest itself now. I was talking to a counselor the other day who said, "That's why they call it *post*-traumatic stress syndrome. It doesn't hit you right away. It comes after."

There are a lot of my friends who are experiencing bad emotional times now, more so than in the last year. Last year they were busy going to funerals and working on the recovery effort and now that's over. And now the city's closing fire departments and there's all the heartache that comes with that and the manner in which that is being done. So there's a lot of baggage that is starting to come out. This is a bad time. And people don't realize that.

# PROJECT NYCOPE

*A continuing effort to contact persons still dealing with the repercussions of 9/11 is called Project NYCope. Established by the Mayor's Office and funded through a grant from the Federal Emergency Management Agency (FEMA), this project assists New York City employees and their families in dealing with the ongoing effects of the disaster. Outreach workers visit offices to describe the counseling services available and*

*reassure people that grief, anxiety and depression are all normal reactions to the stress-*
*ful events of 9/11. Mindy Mount is one of six of the former volunteers from St. Paul's*
*now employed by NYCope.*

## Mindy Mount—There are thousands of people out there who need to know that somebody cares about them.

There were thousands of people who ran from the buildings that day. So we've been going out for months now and talking to them. Really listening to people tell their story. I've met so many people who haven't talked to anyone. We go into people's offices— we've got permission from the commissioners to go to these city offices to talk to their employees. But you're in their space so it's a little bit different. You really have to make yourself vulnerable to go in and talk to people, but what's amazing is that people are so grateful that you've come to see them.

We give people information. A lot of people will say they don't have anything to talk to you about and then they'll talk to you for an hour. We tell people what's available out there in terms of what we can offer: individual counseling, group counseling. Most of the outreach workers are not therapists but we do have therapists on staff who are available for counseling.

I think that God has been preparing me my entire life for these days. I look at it as a huge opportunity and huge gift to be able to go out and listen to people and hear their stories. I wake up every day since 9/11 truly grateful to be alive. I really know in my innermost being that this is the only day I really have, this day! I wake up and ask God to use me. Use me, use me. Use me on the elevator, use me on the street.

Sometimes people ask me to pray with them. It's getting easier to do that. That's never happened to me before. People have asked me recently to talk about my faith and to talk about prayer. When I'm out with people and they bring up prayer, then we talk about it. If they don't, we don't. If they ask what can they do, I answer, "Pray." With where we are right now in our world, I think that's the one thing we can all do.

*Barbara Horn is a Roman Catholic who was born and raised in New York but was in*
*graduate school in Wisconsin on 9/11. Feeling a persistent tug to return to New York,*

*she finally came back at Christmas and volunteered to work at St. Paul's Chapel. Her path was changed by an encounter one night with one of the workers who came up to her (a total newcomer) and said, "I want to thank you because this is my last night here. I wouldn't be here if you all hadn't been here for me all these weeks." "I signed on right there with my life," she said. She moved back to New York and became one of the steady volunteers at St. Paul's. She too has now become one of the outreach workers at NYCope.*

## Barbara Horn—Will fear reign? Or will faith reign?

I'm not looking to repeat the St. Paul's experience but I'm looking to build on it, nourish it. The other day someone referred to us from Project Liberty as part of the healing team. New York has been has been so wounded. There's been so much hurt and woundedness here that there's a certain kind of openness, a fragileness, a tenderness. The recovery, the healing from 9/11 is still happening. While it's still happening, it's still being shaped. And I believe that the more people there are of faith here, to be present and to care, the better and stronger New York will be as it gets back on its feet. People are asking questions they might not have asked, and are asking them in deeper and more searching ways, and are more willing to make changes than ever before. So we can become a model city on how to heal through the effort of community.

St. Paul's has given me the experience of being of service and St. Paul's has positioned me to continue to be of service. And the healing is happening! I still have a lot of questions. I have a few challenges going on—the financial thing. How do I pay the rent? We don't have health benefits at NYCope—or vacations. But I definitely think that because of what's happened, New Yorkers are more open, and open in ways that they wouldn't have been unless they had been so wounded. The healing will depend on what reigns. Will fear reign? Then people will shut down. Or will faith reign? Will support and really caring for each other reign? If that reigns, it's going to be a different New York.

# EMERGENCY MEDICAL SERVICES CHAPLAINS

*In the course of his volunteer work in the Morgue at Ground Zero, the Rev. Stephen R. Harding, a chaplain at Beth Israel Hospital, often found himself working with the Emergency Medical Services personnel. One day he found that though the city provides chaplains for the police and firefighters, no chaplains are provided for the Emergency Medical Services. So Harding has organized volunteers who serve as chaplains to the city's three EMS Battalions in Manhattan. Clergymen Tom Faulkner, John W. Moody, Andrew J.W. Mullins, and Joseph F. Parrish have joined Harding in this ministry. They work in cooperation with the chaplains of the Fire Department. Episcopal Relief and Development has provided some money for training and expenses, but otherwise the chaplains serve as volunteers.*

### Stephen Harding—This was an area of ministry that needed to be done.

I tell myself I'll be there for two hours each week but it always mushrooms into more. I'm there as a presence. The first day I got there, people were talking to me almost non-stop for almost two hours. I've been there enough at this point so that they know me, so when I go back, it's "Where have you been?" The other thing I do there is—I ride on the ambulances. I am there as an observer. I'm not there in any chaplaincy or priestly capacity for the patients. I keep a low profile until we deliver the patient to the hospital, then I talk with the ambulance personnel after we're back in the ambulance. All of us who are doing this have taken at least three courses in critical incident stress management. The latest one included firefighters and police as well as EMS workers and focused on weapons of mass destruction.

*In a similar manner, the Rev. Clayton Crawley, who is currently employed by the Church Pension Fund, has become the chaplain for FireFLAG, the organization of gay and lesbian firefighters. Crawley volunteered regularly at the Morgue during the cleanup period and got to know many of the firefighters on duty at Ground Zero. In the course of this ministry, he discovered that FireFLAG was one group that had no designated chaplain, indeed had many members who were suspicious of any representative of organized religion. The help the chaplains had provided in the grisly work of recovering bodies, however, prompted some members to ask for a chaplain for FireFLAG. Crawley volunteered.*

## Clayton Crawley—It turned out to be a ministry of showing up.

Because they'd never had chaplains before they were extremely suspect, so it turned out to be a ministry of showing up, and for the last six months, I've continued to go to their meetings. At last month's meeting, for the first time, the president looked over and said, "We'd like to invite the chaplain to say a prayer at our meetings from now on; if anyone has a problem with that let me know." It took over six months of being there before they said "Okay you're now a part of us, you can stay here." That's understandable. They got no attention at all as an organization until 9/11. I think for many of them the church is immediately suspect.

In June, 2002, they marched as honorary marshals of the Gay Pride Parade. They wanted a place to change afterwards because they were marching in uniform. I'm an associate at St. Luke in the Fields, so I contacted them, and said, "Can the FireFLAG change clothes there?" They said, "Well, sure, we'll be glad to open the gardens for them and we'll make food." What was amazing was, I was expecting maybe thirty people. We probably had two hundred people from FireFLAG and GOAL (gay and lesbian police) change clothes, and sit in the gardens at St. Luke's. The church had hamburgers and hotdogs and iced tea for them. Just coming out of that church, having them say this meant so much, and it's all of one piece. Coming out of this kind of horrible event, you fast-forward to the end of June and what's happened is here is a group of people who probably have never darkened the door of a church, spend an afternoon enjoying the hospitality and being so surprised by it. It was one of those grace filled moments: being able to stand on the steps, and welcome them into the church!

# ENCOURAGE VOLUNTEERISM

*The powerful experiences of the volunteers at St. Paul's Chapel led to the formation of two separate non-profit groups: the Community Response Foundation and the Nine-Twelve Community. Though both groups are still in a formative stage, each is dedicated to encouraging the development of volunteer activities based on the St. Paul's model. Martin Cowart and Katherine Avery described some of the plans for the Nine-Twelve Community.*

### Katherine Avery—There was a tremendous amount of pain that was still there.

When St. Paul's closed, I realized that our jobs had just begun. There was a tremendous amount of pain that was still there and to me very present and almost urgent in the sense that people didn't want to let go of what had happened to them, and couldn't. The other part of it was I didn't want to let go of what I'd seen humanity do. I didn't want that to stop just because it no longer had St. Paul's Chapel to function in. I wanted to figure out a way to keep that going. I didn't want to think that once the doors closed, we would just go back to normal, to doing what we did before. I don't think any of us will ever be able to go back to the way it was before. So I want to find a way to create a space where people can feel as comfortable as they did at St. Paul's being exactly who they are supposed to be and loving themselves and the people that they are serving.

### Martin Cowart—We must talk about the human issues of rebuilding Manhattan.

We could put together a series of events down here, bringing in the volunteers who experienced what we experienced at St. Paul's as facilitators and invite in the people who live and work in lower Manhattan to come into dialogue to talk about the human issues around rebuilding lower Manhattan, not just the pragmatic issues about the size of the buildings or how much memorial space there's going to be, but how is it going to feel as human beings to relate and work and indeed gather down here. Because when you go to the public hearings, what you hear is two conversations: the Lower Manhattan Development Corporation talking about their plans and which plan is accessible and blah, blah, blah. And then you hear people talking about all the human issues and all their pain. You've got two conversations going on. So if we could provide the place where people could actually come and talk about the *human* issues that are at stake down here in a platform where they would truly be heard, then, I think, we could begin to help heal this area. That's one of our visions.

We've also talked to the Mayor's office about cooperating with Project Cope. They have a social worker who will help us put together a series of art therapy workshops for children. Art is one of the best means for children and adults to process trauma. So the idea is for us to collaborate with Project Cope. They're going to bring in an art therapy teacher who will use our space and gather a class of children from the neighborhood buildings. We will put on the class together. We've also been talking with Ann Webster, who's a psychiatrist, about putting together a support group for mothers in Battery Park City and see how that may evolve.

## Katherine Avery—We must be flexible and ready to change.

What is important to about this process is that as we get closer to it, always in the back of our minds, is the understanding that it is going to change. I mean, even when we get to a point when we can say, "Okay, this is it. This is what we are going to do right now," all of us realize that every couple of months we have to check back in with the people to see if that is really what they need. Just like we have changed, that's going to change. In order for this group to stay alive, it's going to have to change as well.

*Diane Reiners and Carter Booth outlined their hopes for the Community Response Foundation.*

**Diane Reiners—Volunteering can change the world.**

I really believe that volunteering can change the world. So part of what we do is pass on that message. And another part is to go into corporations and say, "You know, if you create a strong volunteer base, do you know how good it is for your company?" I heard back from corporations who volunteered as a group at St. Paul's. They said it helped cross socio-economic and religious and racial barriers by bringing people together to volunteer. So our foundation could help that along.

**Carter Booth—We want to create a space where people can connect.**

One of the strengths of what was happening at St. Paul's was all about people coming together. So we asked, "How do we stay together as a resource for other people, to help *them*?" This experience has been so meaningful for so many people that it's something people want to go back to, to revisit the temporary community that no longer exists *here*. It's gone, but one of the things that can be created is a space where people can reconnect, and that's a different time for everybody, a different place. That's something we realized—that we can create something that can go forward for as long as it is needed, a place where people can come back to talk about those experiences.

# SEPTEMBER 11, 2002

*September 11, 2002 was a solemn day of mourning and remembrance. At a memorial platform erected at Ground Zero, the name of each person who died there was read aloud, the cadence of amplified names wafting into the air above the mass of family members and visitors who crowded the sidewalks and blocked-off streets with a steady funereal beat. The crowds were quiet, many were tearful, often gathered in family clusters that trembled as a particular name was intoned.*

*St. Paul's Chapel opened at eight A.M., newly cleaned and refurbished, the walls and balcony supporting only a select few of the many banners and posters that had hung there for so many months. An exhibit, designed by Lynn Brewster, Manager of Design and Production at Trinity, detailed the volunteer ministry that occupied that space from September 15, 2001 until June 1, 2002 filled the side aisles. Visitors were waiting outside when the door opened, and the crowd grew markedly as the day progressed. Rescue workers who had found solace in that place brought their families, as did many of the volunteers. Hugs and laughter marked chance reunions. Other people simply sat silently weeping in the pews. Every half-hour a bell was rung; a volunteer from the congregation said a prayer and a moment of silence was kept.*

*Music and worship marked the "Day of Hope and Healing" at Trinity Church. At 11:00 A.M., an overflowing congregation was on hand to greet the Archbishop of Canterbury and the Lord Mayor of London, who came to present a large bell, inscribed "To the greater glory of God and in recognition of the enduring links between the City of London and the City of New York. Forged in adversity, September 11, 2001." Archbishop Carey deftly connected London's gift with the significance of the day in his sermon, a few selections of which follow.*

## Archbishop George L. Carey—"No man is an island entire of itself."

Reflecting on what more this bell might symbolize, I was reminded of those extraordinary, resonant lines of the great seventeenth century poet and priest, John Donne, "No man is an island entire of itself, ...every man is a piece of the continent, a part of the main; any man's death diminishes me, because I am involved in mankind; and therefore never send to know for whom the bell tolls; it tolls for thee."

What a remarkable challenge to our shared humanity those words remain today.... And how powerfully they connect, I believe, with two of the ideas we have already touched upon—vulnerability and solidarity. "Any man's death diminishes me, because I am involved in mankind." We are vulnerable because we are all connected, Donne is telling us.

The interconnectedness of our modern world is, in a superficial sense, something of a commonplace.... But Donne is talking about something more; not simply our interconnectedness but also our interdependence: the interdependence of the whole human family—every one of us made in the image of God, made to reflect God's glory. Because, as the Good Samaritan in our New Testament reading recognized so completely, like it or not, we are involved in one another, caught up in one another's sufferings and joys, triumphs and tribulations. And this is as true of nations as it is of individuals; we belong together and we can only truly flourish when we are living in the light of that truth.

Now, it's perhaps when we feel most vulnerable that we may find it the hardest to embrace this challenge of interdependence. At times when we want above all to feel safe and secure, there is a temptation to draw back rather than engage, to cut ourselves off, to retreat behind walls that we may wish to believe are impregnable.

Or, we may be tempted to seek to override others, to lash out in revenge and frustration, and that urge may be especially strong when we believe we have not only right but also might on our side.... But surely the test of true greatness for peoples and nations must be that they are motivated by what should be done, not by what could be done?

How we seek to do that at any time is at the heart of the moral choices that we continually face and make as human beings. And the United States, with its immense potential to make a difference in the world, faces the daunting challenge of wielding power and influence with others in ways that do justice to the vision of our shared humanity and fate as expressed by John Donne.... As they face this great challenge, the leaders of this nation deserve our fervent and sincere prayers.

But that challenge is certainly not alien to the spirit or understanding of your founding fathers. For it's on a Christian understanding of the equality and dignity of all human beings, of both the potential and the limits of human power, that America has grown up over the centuries and continues to proclaim today "In God we trust." That trust, and the moral tradition which has flowed from it, are both the beginning and the best of America.

That is the basis on which to believe that on September the eleventh in years to come, we shall be able both to remember the past and to affirm the present. We shall be able to believe that, by the grace of God Almighty, the hope that has risen so courageously from the ashes of twelve months ago will have strengthened our commitment to make this vulnerable world a place of true and lasting security—a place where God's goodness and bounty are shared by everyone.

# 6
## REFLECTIONS

What profit is there in my blood, if I go down to the Pit?
will the dust praise you or declare your faithfulness?
—Psalm 30, Book of Common Prayer

## GROUND ZERO SPIRITUALITY

The Rev. Dr. J. Robert Wright, Historiographer of the Episcopal Church, has written that "we who live as Christians today must not be content merely to study the history of the past, we must also collaborate in creating the history of the future."

In the crucible of Ground Zero, we believe that a spirituality was forged that can sustain us in the new world born on 9/11. The shock and horror of the initial attack and the tremendous destruction in its aftermath melded with the grueling months of searching through rubble for human remains and with the generous outpouring of love and concern from thousands of volunteers from many parts of the world to produce this spirituality. The tremendous synergy of the nine months after 9/11 pushed us back to the basic elements of our traditional faith, elements that proved to be resilient and reliable. Confronted with our own vulnerability, we found strength and comfort in serving each other. Religious patterns and practices took on new meaning in the shadow of the destroyed towers. It was as if we tested the very basis on which our faith was built—and it held strong.

What have the voices in this book said to us about Ground Zero spirituality? What wisdom can we glean from their experience? In this final chapter, we hope to suggest some of the outlines of the spirituality that is emerging from Ground Zero. These are

tentative suggestions, for the elements in the Ground Zero crucible that are still bub-
bling. The overwhelming agreement among those who were interviewed is that this
process is not over. We continue to live and relive in our minds the events of the days
since 9/11. What is Ground Zero spirituality? The testimony of the voices published
here suggests it might include the following themes.

## Vulnerability

The Rev. Stuart Hoke articulated the sense of spiritual vulnerability felt by many in
the months after 9/11.

> I have never in my life felt both a physical and emotional and a spiritual
> sense of evisceration. I felt cut up, all my defenses went down.
> Emotions I didn't know I had came out. I would clump them together,
> primarily grief and fear, and working on those the entire year, and on
> after the first year. I define the post-9/11 spiritual vulnerability as the
> following: loss of illusion, loss of the sense of safety, then the fear that
> this could happen again.
>
> But there is the potential of spiritual renewal in all of this. September
> 11 greatly affected me, but I've known beyond a shadow of a doubt,
> even if I died the next day, even if we have another terrorist attack
> tomorrow, that great things have happened for me as a result of this.
> That's had to do with willingness to offer God my suffering and to line
> it up with God's suffering. So I don't know how I've learned recovery,
> it certainly hasn't been from a textbook, but it has been not only from
> experience, but also from reflection on experience. What one author
> called "creative brooding," brooding, ruminating over a period of time,
> and the learning emerges, adding to my conversion, and transforming
> me, and staying with me.

Hoke's testimony is important in defining a new understanding of the Christian
acceptance of change, both personal and historical. It suggests that what we, as American
Christians, were taught on 9/11 is that in order for God's realm to be established on the
face of this earth, the old order must crumble, dissolve, disintegrate, before the new one
is forged. Dissolution is positive; upheaval means we are going somewhere. We are not
empty ciphers whirling about an empty universe, God is involved.

When structures and forms and ways of adapting and even very personal survival techniques no longer serve us, God makes a very distinct and powerful appearance in our lives in order to do away with the old and establish the new. Disintegration, dissolution and collapse are signs heralding a new freedom. They are hallmarks of God's inscrutable technique for redeeming time. They are harbingers of a new way of life hitherto unimagined.

Archbishop Rowan Williams agrees that this is the great lesson of 9/11. "While it is not a school, which left to ourselves we would have chosen, we are Christians because we believe the school of death is quite simply the only way in which we understand resurrection."

## At a time of tragedy, God is present in the human community and the church.

Carter Booth, who had worked in the financial community, became a volunteer and staff person at Ground Zero and St. Paul's Chapel, said,

> Those who were recovering the body parts in the Pit knew that they could come here to St. Paul's Chapel and see people. That made a difference, that you knew that someone was always available to talk to you, and that made a difference for every single person at one time or another who came through those doors. It was a ministry of presence at St. Paul's that God was definitely there and around. There was a presence of God that included all of the people at work in the chapel. Because of this presence of God through people, I think of Ground Zero as this very special, holy ground. Holy place. Sacred place. And no doubt the people who worked here, the people who came here and worked, the people who gave of themselves also got that feeling of God's presence. Despite the collapse of the towers, which were modern-day structures, the church remains standing, and the church is really the people. They remain standing. They make it God's place here.

Another volunteer at St. Paul's Chapel described God's presence through people in this way:

> For those of you who are here, you feel it, you know it, you go out and tell everybody else what is the living Word of God, and what is the experience of being in the close presence of God's people. It is your hand. It is your love. It is your word. It is your thanks. That's part of the living God. You come to feel that you are an extension of the living God, and this is an overwhelming experience of liberation and affirmation.

The technical theological term for these witnesses of God's presence in the human community is incarnation. The ministry of the Episcopal Church at Ground Zero was thoroughly incarnational. The heart and the soul of this ministry were found in the incarnation of the Word of God in Scripture, liturgy, and human action. The incarnation of God's action to liberate and nurture is not confined to Jesus 2,000 years ago, but has been present among us in the actions of dedicated men and women who gave of themselves sacrificially in 9/11 ministries over the last years.

What is the message of Ground Zero spirituality at this point? It is this: God enters into the material world. God is present at the roots of humanity's natural, bodily life. The fullness of God is revealed not only in the mind and the speech of Jesus but in his physical body, in his actions, in his deeds. What we have learned since 9/11 is that the most basic human experiences of needs, satisfactions, anxieties, and even horror, are the soil, the matter in which the divine can be revealed. Grace shines through, illuminates, and transfigures the natural order, not in part, but in its totality. In the places of the greatest darkness and depravity, God has entered into the processes of both birth and death.

Therefore, in the Anglican tradition particularly, there is a very great affirmation of the goodness of the human, despite its disorder and decay. The human is capable of bearing the divine. Yet Anglicanism must also say something to us about suffering and sorrow, pain and grief, the way forward to sudden death. At Ground Zero, Christianity would not have been much use if it could not speak to and confront the realities of pain and loss, and separation from loved ones.

# PEOPLE HAVE CLAIMED THE BAPTISMAL COVENANT AS THEIR OWN

In the Service of Holy Baptism in the 1979 Book of Common Prayer, the entire congregation is asked to join with those being baptized in affirming the baptismal covenant. That covenant includes the statement of belief contained in the Apostle's Creed and five commitments: to continue in teaching, fellowship, the breaking of bread and prayers; to resist evil and repent; to proclaim the Good News of God in Christ; to serve Christ by loving our neighbors; and to strive for justice and peace. These are the basic commitments that each member of Christ's church makes, and since 1979, members of the Episcopal Church have repeated these words innumerable times. And the message has sunk in. We are all ministers—clergy and laity—equally responsible to live out the baptismal covenant in the world.

The response to the tragedy of 9/11 that we have detailed in this book demonstrates that church members have internalized the baptismal covenant. The laity *knew* they were empowered to respond, as Christ would have responded, to this time of dreadful need. As Mary O'Shaughnessy said,

> The baptismal covenant was something I meditated on throughout my experience in ministry at Ground Zero. Respecting the dignity of every person was for me the way of expressing "get out of the way and let other people give their gifts." In the baptism of a child, there is a phrase about joy and wonder in all God's work. There was joy and wonder in the work of God and the people coming together, and when you are open to that, you find it in places you would never have expected.

The Rev. Daniel Ade agreed.

> People had the sense of, "well I can pick up and go because I'm a representative of the gospel even though I don't have a plastic collar around my neck." That's one of the reasons I think that the ministry of the church flourished at Ground Zero, because there was that foundation that we're all ministers already in place. And people understood that.

The presence of laity revolutionized what was possible in the spiritual response to the terrorist attacks. Lay people identified needs; they responded to those needs. They didn't wait for authorization or permission from clerical or secular authorities. They also knew that the response had to be lovingly offered, wrapped in care and consideration for the person being helped. Realizing that to be effective, the response must be a community response, they depended upon the church to provide that community.

The year after 9/11 demonstrated a potential for mission in radical forms that has rarely been fully realized within the Episcopal Church. Volunteers from many parts of the country who served at Ground Zero returned home to initiate and revitalize local programs. The congregation of St. James Church in Eureka Springs, Arkansas, has invited Jews and Muslims and Buddhists to join them in an ongoing program of interfaith worship and education. From Sheridan, Wyoming, the people of St. Peter's Church take medical and dental care to a rehabilitation center on the southern tip of Mexico. In Spartanburg, South Carolina, an already busy schedule of community outreach programs of the Church of the Advent has been expanded by volunteers who had made the long trek northward to work at St. Paul's Chapel. These and so many other individual efforts demonstrate that an empowered laity is definitely one of the hallmarks of Ground Zero spirituality.

# THE DEEPENING OF ORDAINED MINISTRY

The Rev. Rand Frew, who has been active in social justice ministries in New York City for many years, speaks of the impact of his work at Ground Zero.

> I came to have a deeper appreciation of what I understand the essentials of priesthood to be—to be a sacramental person, to be a sign. A priest is a visible sign of God's presence and God's grace in the world. And a priest is the means by which the sacraments are made available to people in terms of the Eucharist, water for baptism, oil for anointing, and absolution for forgiveness of sins. Those were what people wanted, what they needed, what they looked for. All of this is what a priest had to have his or her ears and eyes and nose and hands pricked up and ready to respond to. My exercise of priesthood strengthened my faith, because I had a strong sense of God's presence with me as I performed sacramental acts. I was actually overwhelmed by the abiding presence of God in this ministry.

Stuart Hoke confirms the same rediscovery of priesthood in the context of generous service to others:

As a priest I feel that I have had an amazing part in our recovery, but it has been in ways that I did not expect. It has been a lot of me as a care-giver, but I have needed care. As a priest I have hurt so much through this thing. I had to pocket my pride as a priest and move in a new mutual direction, working much more closely in relationship with others. I have had to do this in order to survive in this new period after 9/11.

All witnesses testify that priesthood was a key ingredient in the spirituality of 9/11. Throughout the year, the Episcopal Church in all of its various ministries emphasized that the gospel, the Christian mystery takes bodily form, and that this gospel was available to all in need constantly through the ordained ministry. Whatever the public profile, we know that in the ministry at Ground Zero, people welcomed priests and deacons and members of religious orders. They honored those people as those who are entrusted with the task of welcoming God's people into God's presence, and offering them God's hospitality in a real, concrete, tangible, converting form that was sacramental and longed for by rescue workers.

At Ground Zero the Christian sacraments made God's holiness findable. And wher-ever the holy was made available for those in need, ordained persons received a new awareness that those who handle holy things on behalf of the people of God must be mindful of the awesomeness of the mystery, the need for consecration of life for the task, and the support of the community to bear this burden.

In the midst of this crisis precipitated by the terrorists' attacks, there was a new under-standing of the importance of both lay and ordained roles in the church, a new sense of balance and of the need to find ways to strengthen people to fill those roles, so that they could be worthy vehicles for God's grace for the whole people of God. The object of the whole exercise of ministry at Ground Zero was not emphasis on the particular vehicles of God's grace, but rather on the determination that God should be present with God's people, that all should get a foretaste of the promised horizon of heaven.

# RADICAL HOSPITALITY

The Rev. Lyndon Harris who directed the ministry at St. Paul's Chapel spoke of the concept of radical hospitality as a means by which this balance of lay and ordained roles could be achieved, providing a space in which both forms of ministry could flourish, and all people would be welcome.

> Radical hospitality meant that we did not give the impression that we were to receive anything back. It was true hospitality, giving without any anticipation of return, giving for the sake of giving. I think that was one of the most important things about the ministry of St. Paul's Chapel. What I saw was that there was reciprocity of gratitude that took place at St. Paul's. People would outdo one another in showing love. It really was a love feast! People were encouraged and supported and empowered to do this fierce work they were doing. Part of the definition of radical hospitality at St. Paul's was that the structure of ministry was bottom-up, outside-in, and that's what made it so alive. I don't know how you routine-ize that, how you institutionalize such a form of hospitality, but this is obviously a structural key to the kind of spirituality that was associated with St. Paul's Chapel.

Harris is clear that the foundation of radical hospitality at St. Paul's was the concept of Christian love. The foundation of this love was the practice of daily, ordinary loving of all the Ground Zero workers who came to St. Paul's to be sustained. Such hospitality wasn't always easy; it required of the volunteers the practice of patience, imagination, and good humor.

Love, trust, acceptance—these are the things the staff of St. Paul's tried to share with unambiguous generosity. And they were enhanced by a spiritual dimension. The leadership group worked at their primary relationship with Christ. Though people of all faiths, and of no faith, were welcomed at St. Paul's, it was through this growing relationship with Christ that links were forged with others, so that the leadership community grew toward maturity in loving, and in the giving and receiving of love.

Expanding on his definition of radical hospitality, Harris explained,

> First of all, I would say that holiness includes and is built on wholeness. What we tried to offer at St. Paul's was an integrated approach to min-

istry where all the needs of the human being were taken into consideration. Wholeness is very much at the heart of holiness, and that is one reason why we were so influential in the relief effort, because we were able to embrace the whole person.

In our approach at St. Paul's we paid attention to the needs of the body. We did not set up prayer stations like some of the fundamentalists. We had massage therapists praying with their hands. We had chiropractors. We insisted on saying that the love of Christ is extravagant. We tried to embody that extravagant love at St. Paul's. We didn't serve bologna sandwiches. We had the finest food we could get our hands on.

So ultimately "radical hospitality" pointed to a ministry that took the body seriously. This ministry of the body then became another defining characteristic of Ground Zero spirituality.

# THE BODY

Clergy who served as volunteers in the Pit and the Morgue speak of the importance of the body and resurrection in shaping the experience of ministering at Ground Zero. The Rev. Tom Synan, from the Church of the Heavenly Rest in Manhattan, who spent much time blessing body parts in the Pit.

I wanted to stress a form of belief that was re-emphasized through my whole experience of working in the Pit and working with bodies, and that was the concept of the resurrection of the body. I mean that is the central affirmation of the Christian faith that became a central affirmation to me again through my work at Ground Zero.

The Rev. Tom Faulkner, of St. James Church in Manhattan, worked for nine months as a chaplain at the Morgue and speaks of his new understanding of the reality of death.

As clergy, we deal with dead bodies. We're in hospitals. We might be visiting families in which someone has died, maybe a parishioner, maybe the relative of a parishioner. We're sometimes called to the scenes of accidents and death in home or in industry, or in business. So, it's not that we're unused to dead bodies. We are. We're used to dead bodies. But here there were dead bodies unlike any we'd ever seen before.

The only analogy really is warfare. One of my chaplains was a seventy-three-year-old Roman Catholic priest from Inwood, who did two tours in Vietnam. What he said to me so clearly was that what we're looking at is remains. That's exactly it. They're remains. There is no spirit here. The spirit is with God. This is dust. The dust we come from. The dust we're going back to. We're told that. But this was so clearly the case that there wasn't ever for me an aspect of the work of blessing that was disagreeable because of the nature of the human remains at which I was looking.

That brought the realization that what we are, in terms of our best, is: we're spirit, that God indwells us, and when we're in touch with that, when we're in touch with the spirit in each other, life has abundance and has meaning.

The Rev. Gayanne Silver who serves at Trinity Church discussed the importance of ashes for the families of victims.

When Trinity was open, people started coming in asking for ashes from the churchyard because they had lost someone and they didn't want to take the ashes from the street. They wanted the ashes that were around the church. What was important to them was the symbolism of the body turned to ash, but how do you pray when the bodies are in such a state? Trying to pray for thousands of people in rubble, that is a different kind of prayer that none of us are used to saying.

Central to understanding Ground Zero spirituality is this confrontation with the reality of the importance of the body in understanding our identity, even our identity at the moment of death and a certain hard realism about what happens next. The centrality of this theme was highlighted at the Trinity Church service on September 11, 2002. The anthem at that service was Herbert Howells' setting of this text of Prudentius, the fourth century Latin Christian poet, a text which captures completely this aspect of 9/11 spirituality.

Take him, earth, for cherishing, to thy tender breast receive him.
Body of a man I bring thee, noble even in its ruin.
Once was this a spirit's dwelling, by the breath of God created.
High the heart that here was beating. Christ the prince of all its living.
Guard him well, the dead I give thee,
Not unmindful of His creature shall He ask it;
He who made it symbol of His mystery.

What was confronted at Ground Zero was a basic fact of Christian faith: the expectation that the body returns at the end of time, that the person is not only an immortal soul but also a psychosomatic unity. The body is crucial to the identity and to the spiritual life of the person. Ground Zero spirituality is radically positive in that it recognizes in the crucified and risen Christ the power to transform the body. The church, by pointing to its risen Lord, points the way toward the realization of a new humanity, a representation of the God of love, and a realization of future hope.

The resurrection of Jesus certifies that God's commitment to the world does not end with the death of each one of us, or of Jesus himself. In his resurrection, Jesus is the true man, the representative of all humanity. Through the action of raising Jesus from the dead, God assures all people that the final word of God to the human race is life. Christ's presence at the church's Eucharistic table is another sign that he is abroad in the world, ready to bring new life to every heart and home. The spirituality of the body naturally points to a central role for the Eucharist and the liturgy in the spiritual response to 9/11.

## The Body—Eucharist and Liturgy

The Rev. Win Peacock, Director of John Heuss House, has made an important connection between the emphasis on the body and a Eucharistic theology.

> Those of us who remained in lower Manhattan breathed the air, and because the air contained the ash of the individuals who were incinerated on 9/11, we began to think theologically through what that meant to breathe. And we began to take seriously the words of Jesus when he mystically assigned to the least of his brethren, attributes that he had earlier assigned to himself. So if Jesus is indeed mystically identified with the least of his brethren, if you are breathing the ash in lower

Manhattan, if the cells of individuals are now becoming a part of your own molecular biology, are you not indeed participating in the Eucharist, as equally valid as when an ordained person consecrates the bread and the wine and distributes these elements to the members of the congregation? Were we not being fed by the body and blood of One Jesus of Nazareth, the Son of God, as we were breathing in the ash of those who died on 9/11?

At Ground Zero, Christ-Eucharist-People of God came to be seen essentially as one mystery through which the liberating power of God was unleashed to restore the dignity of men and women caught in dehumanizing circumstances. Bread and wine, the human community gathered at the Lord's Table, these elements came to be seen as the focal point of the renewal of the earthly life of God's people. In the simple act of eating and drinking, at St. Paul's and at other post-9/11 centers, God was seen to take these elements of daily food, these social acts of eating and drinking as instruments of building up human solidarity and human connectedness.

Kenneth Leonczyk, who began working on the bucket brigade in the Pit on 9/11, testified,

> For me spiritually it was powerful. Everything became sacramental because we were dealing with our bodies—the whole body and blood thing was very real. We could be killed at any moment by a falling building. There was blood everywhere. We were dealing with our own blood. There was jagged metal all over the place—we were getting cut. In the idea of the sacramental body and blood, what's very important about that is it's there, it's corporeal, it's tangible. When we do the Eucharist, it's not just something we think about. For me, there was a human solidarity.

Participation in the daily Eucharist at St. Paul's Chapel also pointed in another direction: to our own participation in Christ's death.

Presiding Bishop Frank Griswold, summarized this theme of Ground Zero theology and spirituality in this moving testimony about his visit to the disaster site on the Feast of the Holy Cross, September 14, 2001.

> What struck me particularly several days after the attack on 9/11 was the power within the Eucharistic liturgy to ground us in situations where

otherwise we would feel at a loss, vulnerable, confused. On September 14, I came to Ground Zero and found myself first at the Seamen's Church Institute, one of the Episcopal institutions of the Diocese of New York, and I was celebrating the Eucharist. It turned out to be the Feast of the Holy Cross. In the course of the liturgy the reading is one in which Jesus says, "When I am lifted up from the earth, I will draw all people, all things to myself."

That text settled somewhere in the back of my consciousness. On the way back I passed by St. Paul's Chapel. A fine dust covered everything in the chapel, but as I left the church I noticed above the altar the small brass crucifix with arms extended, and suddenly the text "when I am lifted up" came to me vividly. These tiny brass arms contained all the horror, anger, confusion and grief that existed at Ground Zero only one block away. Here was a place where people of faith could stand, unifying ourselves with the One who could embrace everything, even the worst that could happen to us. That is why I say the liturgy of the Episcopal Church can be incredibly grounding, even in the most disorienting circumstances.

# CONNECTEDNESS

The action of relief work and the action of the Eucharist were ultimately the same, to create a new connectedness, to create a new sense of human linkage and unity out of what had been alienation, disaster and chaos.

Stuart Hoke recalled,

> Boundaries evaporated in this environment. Class distinctions, social distinctions, racial distinctions, they were all unheard of amidst this action of worship and this action of work. We had a volunteer team from a very prominent church in Greenwich, Connecticut, serving alongside a skinhead, leather-jacketed team of motorcyclists from Los Angeles. They bonded for life. I hear they still write to one another. At Christmastime several Jewish and Muslim congregations offered to take over the facility so that Christians could go to midnight mass. Even Sikh

congregations from all over the country sent checks to help out. Ecumenism usually comes from above. This time it came from the grassroots up. This time it worked.

The coordinator of chaplains at the Morgue, Tom Faulkner, explained,

> We were having conversations with people, spiritual conversations, with very closed communities like the fire department and the police department and the emergency medical services. There was a sacredness to our connectedness with these people, very unique, coupled with the fact that we were connecting in a way that spoke about what the human community could be. If we could do this here where it didn't matter if you were black, or gay, or a cop, or a construction worker—whether you were Muslim, Greek Orthodox, Roman Catholic, whether you'd served in Vietnam or fought against Vietnam—it didn't make any difference. We were gathered together in a community doing sacred work.

This experience of building community at Ground Zero, the connectedness that is a part of 9/11 spirituality, can serve to inspire not only the Episcopal Church, but also the Anglican Communion as a whole, to be an instrument of human community around the globe at this moment of alienation and vulnerability. The Archbishop of Canterbury, Rowan Williams, defined this mission in his Hobart lecture in New York on September 12, 2001 at the Cathedral of St. John the Divine, saying,

> Because in all this, in trying to understand pastoral work as something death teaches, we're saying that in the Christian community, the taking up of risk by everyone for the sake of Jesus Christ is actually the distinctive thing that we're here for. And if we ever want to answer any questions about what the authentic church looks like, maybe the simplest way that we can begin to ask is, is this a community that takes Christ-like risks?

# RESURRECTION

We began this book with words from sermons on dust preached by a bishop 1,500 years ago after the destruction of the City of Rome in 410. We end with words from contemporary preacher, the Rev. Barbara C. Crafton, who was serving as rector of St. Clement's Church, Manhattan, when the Twin Towers fell. This passage calls to mind the words of Abraham Lincoln who sought to find meaning for the future of the United States in the cruel tally of the dead at Gettysburg. Lincoln looked back to the founding principles of the American Republic and recast them as the basis for a liberating hope in the new historical context which he could perceive beyond the blood sacrifice of the Civil War. Crafton looks back to the fundamental fact of the Christian faith, belief in the resurrection, as the source of that hope which will carry us forward as individuals and community as we continue to make our spiritual response to 9/11.

> There's a really tacky bit of the kind of office art that circulates after any significant event. One of the pieces that made the rounds, and I think is still making the rounds, is a very crude drawing of the two towers with smoke and debris coming up in a cloud from them. On the top of the cloud are all these little figures. They're the dead. And above all this— is Jesus with his arms open in a wide embrace. It is very crude. Hopelessly sentimental. But actually, it's the truth! That is what happened. Boom! Right to Heaven they went. Immediate. I think that people, because they need to, are grasping at the openness of God's love, a childish hope of Heaven. My hope of Heaven is very childish. It doesn't differ materially from that crude drawing that has made the rounds.
>
> For us, death looks like the end. But I think that, when so many people have died all at once, we are forced to ask ourselves, "Well, is it really the end? Or is it a moment along a continuum, a widening of a life that actually. Our life here is going to look real narrow when we go there. We're very divided. We have all kinds of regulations about barriers and things. And they don't have any of it. They don't even have the barrier of time.
>
> And, so, they are more present with us now than they were when they were here. So you dream of them. You hear their song. You see somebody who walks like them. A million things bring them back, never, at least in the early years, without a dagger through your heart, but also

never increasingly without gratitude that you had them at all, and without the suspicion that they are with us in some way.

And to me, more and more, the older I get, the closer I get to going over there, the more evidence, satisfying only to me, I'll admit, but evidence I see that life goes on. Not this life. And we might wish it were. But life, nonetheless. I believe that more and more.

Our experience of the bombing acquired a liturgical cadence. It became a story. And it's a story that we witnessed and know what happened. We saw it. I saw the buildings burn. That's a matter of historical record in my memory. So we understand that. I may still not be able to believe it happened. But I saw it, and it's part of my experience. The resurrection. We don't see it. Understanding the resurrection is not going to happen. It's a mystery. We have what happened as history in the past. And we tell it so it can remain in the present. But the resurrection is the inbreaking of the future into our life now.

The event of the resurrection is full of mystery and misunderstandings. We can't encompass a thing like that in the world of experience. But we do know death. We can talk about death. We hang back before the risen Christ because we do not understand him and because our sorrow blinds us. The dust of it gets in our eyes and in our mouths and throats and all over us so that we even smell like it. Our protective gear doesn't really protect us. "We are unprotected and unprotectable," a man told me the other day, and he was right. And we linger over the drawing of Jesus sweeping up the dead in his arms of love, thousands of them, all at once, longing for it to be true. I think it is true. I know it is. I know it.